Readymade Speeches

for all occasions

W. A. Whiteman

GOODWILL PUBLISHING HOUSE
New Delhi-110008 • **INDIA**

Published by
Rajneesh Chowdhry
for
GOODWILL PUBLISHING HOUSE
B-9, Rattan Jyoti, 18, Rajendra Place
New Delhi-110008
Tel. : 5750801, 5755519
Fax : 91-5763428

© Publisher

All rights reserved. No part of this publication may be reproduced, stored in a retrieval system, or transmitted in any form or by any means, electronic, mechanical, photocopying, recording or otherwise, without the prior permission of the publishers.

PREFACE

Speech has a great power. Many professional skills depend on this power. The lawyer wins cases, the salesman sells products, the dictator rules over his subjects with his hypnotic speech-power.

The preceptor turns the minds of his disciples to veracity, the professor wins the hearts of his students, and the extraordinary orator creates pin drop silence in the audience to turn people's minds on the right path.

A speech is to be made up, the speaker should have it ready, but the born speaker forgets his written matter, veers from documented words, merges himself heart and soul in his speech, gives vent to his feelings, his obsession his verve, and creates fire works, the sparks of which lit up all the corners of the darkened souls.

A speaker has to reach his audience, his public, and the method and means by which he does it, is his own. He has to bring out his individually through his speech, so that his image stands separate from that of others.

CONTENTS

Section I. INTRODUCTION

Section II. SPEECHES ON TOPICS

1. Upliftment Of Children — 7
2. Violence To Women — 10
3. National Students Union — 13
4. Lawyers' Convention — 16
5. Science And Development — 19
6. Business Meeting — 22
7. National Seminar On Teachers — 25
8. Political Party's Annual Conference — 27
9. Conference On Human Rights — 30
10. Environment And Mankind — 33
11. Banking Development — 35
12. Programme On Health — 38
13. Economic Planning — 41
14. Human Resource Development — 44
15. Election Success — 46

Section III. CEREMONIES

1. Marriage Anniversary — 51
2. Marriage Engagement — 53
3. Birthday Party — 55
4. Birthday Celebrations — 57
5. Religious Ceremony (Christmas) — 58
6. Diwali Celebrations — 60

(v)

7.	Welcome Speech	62
8.	Farewell Speech	63
9.	Student's Annual Day	64

Section IV. OFFICIAL OCCASIONS

1.	Shareholders' Meeting	69
2.	Board Of Directors' Meeting	70
3.	Another Board Of Directors' Meeting	72
4.	Delegation's Visit	73
5.	Welcoming Delegations	75
6.	Felicitation	77
7.	Condolence Meeting	78
8.	On Receipt Of Award	79
9.	Inauguration Of Function (Cultural Meet)	81
10.	Inauguration Of Trade Exhibition	82
11.	Presiding Over Annual Function Of Association	84

Section V. SITUATIONS

1.	Picnic	87
2.	Banquet Toast	89
3.	Club Meeting	90
4.	Welfare Society	92
5.	Get-Together	93
6.	Cocktail Speech	94
7.	After-Dinner Speech of the Host	95
8.	Post-Dinner Speech Of the Guest	96

Section VI. MISCELLANEOUS

1.	Children's Society (Secretary's Speech)	99
2.	Ladies Meeting	101
3.	Soccer Championship	103

4.	On Joining as Manager of a Company	105
5.	On Taking-Over As Secretary of Labour Union	107
6.	On Taking-Over As Association Presidentship	108
7.	Addressing A Press Conference	110
8.	On Joining As College Principal	113
9.	Charity Performance (Secretary's Speech)	115
10.	Vote Of Thanks	116
11.	Motor Rally	117
12.	Fashion Parade	119
13.	Beauty Contest	121

Section VII. DEBATE

1.	A Debate On Divorce	125

Section VIII. EXERCISES

1.	Democracy Versus Socialism (An Outline)	131
2.	Industry Versus Agriculture (An Outline)	131
3.	Urban And Rural Life Styles (An Outline)	131
4.	Retiring Person's Speech (An Outline)	131
5.	Film Award (Best Actress) (An Outline)	132

SECTION I
INTRODUCTION

1
Introduction

A speech is a composition of words, but it is different from other compositions. A speech is built up with spoken words. An essay is made up of written words. If an essay is read as a speech, it could be at best regarded as a message, but not a proper speech.

A good word or expression which is written, can be read over and over again, but not so, in the case of a speech. Words and expression uttered in a speech mostly melt in the air unless treasured in the minds of some among the audience.

The speaker, therefore, has to hammer literally in his point on the audience. He has to repeat his words his expressions, he has to take to rhetoric, to alliteration, to dramatisation. But not dramatisation of his point of view. He has to blow up his reasoning with shouts and enthusiasm, so that the minds of the audience ring out with his arguments with the echoes of their sounds.

Just as he inflates his own points with one disdainful crunching sound, he has to, and he can, crush the other side's favourite points.

One has to have some training in speech-making. It is not the kind of training that one can get in a class-room, but if one has the will and interest to become a speaker, then one should begin one's apprenticeship by listening to speeches, by attending meetings and gatherings where speeches are made.

A person, thus, has to judge which speeches are good and impressive and which are not. He can then analyse why the good speeches are impressive. Then he himself has to weigh the effects of his uttered words. He can practise his speech in his room, and his resounding words would tell him, what effects his words would create.

Certainly, most good speakers are born with an inherent capacity for speech-making. But others can also follow their footsteps and become great speakers, if they capture the art of identifying themselves with the issue, the topic or the subject on which they are delivering the speech.

One may learn the speech by heart, but if one exactly reproduces the speech, as learnt, it would be ineffective. While delivering the learnt speech, as one gets into the heat of one's arguments, one would utter different words and expressions, as well as act and make postures, which would at once impress the audience and there would be automatic response of clappings and applause.

When a person stands on the dais to deliver a speech, he has to either support the issue or reject it. In a debate this is firmly marked, and a person cannot take up a position in-between. In delivering a speech, however, he can choose a middle path, but in that case he has to show both the sides in their true colour.

For instance, while speaking on the subject like free mixing of boys and girls, or the good and bad of divorce, the speaker can blend the pros and cons of the issue to conclude that moderate mixing of boys and girls would take the steam off their curiosity, and pave the way for their healthy growth. Similarly, a divorce once in a while, may be good to save a woman's life and place her on the path of hope. But, the speaker has to, first of all, present the extreme evils and merits in both these cases.

To produce the most lasting effect on the audience, is one of the main objectives of delivering a speech. A speech may be effective for a short while, that is, as long as it lasts. Or, a speech may have a deeper and lasting effect on the audience.

When a speaker blows up his arguments unnecessarily with shouts and dramatics, he may succeed in holding the attention of his audience, but this effect might not be soul-stirring.

Deep-rooted effects are created by a speech which has the speech-histrionics, but is backed also by sound reasonings and arguments. It needs no mentioning that the speaker's efforts should be creating lasting effects.

SECTION II
SPEECHES ON TOPICS

1
Upliftment of Children

Mr. Chairman, Honourable Chief Guest, Ladies and Gentlemen!

I am glad to say today a few words on the subject which is of vital importance to us, to our society, to our nation and civilisation.

Children are the buds that must be merged to bloom in full and when these do so, when these buds, the future hopeful of our generation, open up fully, to display their grandeur and distribute their fragrance, all around, society is complete.

Ladies and Gentlemen, these are no new things. These matters are known to all. Our generation has to provide all the facilities and opportunities to our children. This is not only our duty, but this is their basic right as well. Otherwise, we as parents have no right to bring them into this world, to expose them to the hazards and hardships of this world, without giving them the initial protection that they need.

If we put a small flower plant in our garden or in a pot, we have to water it daily and regularly, apply plant-nourishing things like fertilizers, spray pesticide, etc. to facilitate the plant's continuous and unobstructed growth.

What we would do to a simple plant, should we or would we not do for a child, which is the very replica of our blood and soul. And just think, ladies and gentlemen! how vulnerable a child is, how dependent it is on the parents, guardians or those are in charge of their welfare.

These small saplings, these children, how tender in feelings they are, how vulnerable, how desiring and requiring attention and care, how weak they are and how impressionable !

The children, that is some children would grow, no doubt, without any assistance whatsoever, just as many wild flowers and plants grow in the woods even through the weeds. But the tender hearts of these children, their finer feelings, and in fact all the good things and sensitiveness of the mind and soul that grow naturally to culminate in fruition, are apt to be blunted, restrained, checked, crushed.

The outcome of growth without care, may be good, it may be terrible. The neglected and exploited children could grow in them the determination to rise and shine and to be bigger and far bigger than others. There have been industrialists and other successful men whose childhood had been spent in the worst frustration.

On the other hand, it is but natural that such dejected and deprived children would develop in them a universal antagonism against the settled systems of the world, and would seek the demolish every good order to be substituted by vile actions, which could be the reflections of their distorted thoughts. These children would therefore, grow upto become anti-social elements and even criminals whose only target in the life could be to wreck the face of civilisation. They would utlimately become the dregs of society, its polluted, unwanted and abhored section. But whom should we blame for that ? The blame is to fall on us, we who are the parents, and we who proclaim ourselves as the guardians of society, civilisation and culture.

Ladies and Gentlemen, these facts are not unknown to you, and idle deliberations and discussions will land us nowhere. Every moment that we spend in unfruitful thought, could be vital for a child to turn it from the evil path or to prod and push it (child) to the goals of achievement.

Every moment is precious. We have to shake ourselves out of inertia and inaction and divert all our efforts to concrete and productive channels, so that we can save the lives of unpriviledged children of our land from a desperate destiny. The developed countries of the world are urged to contribute one percent of their national income towards assisting the developing countries, in the framework of UN Cooperation.

We may also make some such rule for contribution per family. Even a very normal amount, monthly or yearly, might build up a large sum of money, which could be utilized for the maintenance and career build-up of so many hapless children.

Many Governments of the world are now aware of the great treasure that is confined in human resources. Proper development and application of such resources, the judicious mobilization of the same would provide a nation the reservoir of man-power which would enrich a nation's temporal and ethical status in the unity of nations. Let us not forget poet Wordsworth's words "The child is the father of man".

Thank you.

2
Violence to Women

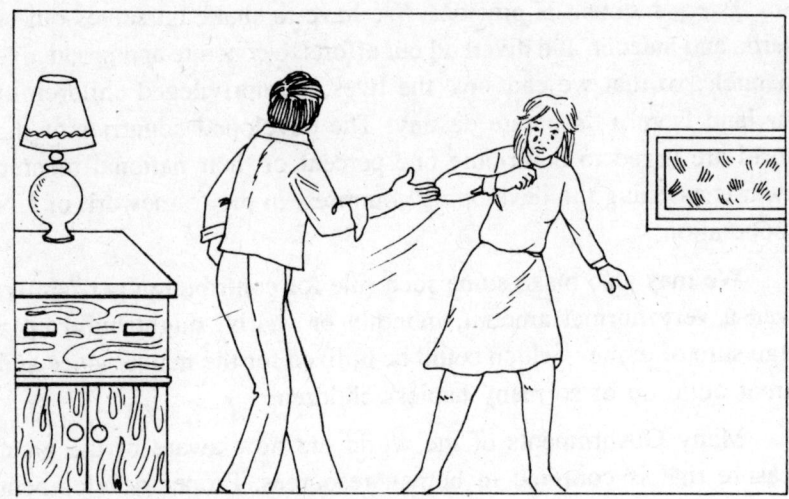

Mr. Chairman, Ladies and Gentlemen !

It is great honour for me that I have got this opportunity to present to you my views on a matter that is one of the main social ills of our society. This matter or the situation is 'violence to women'.

We should feel much pains and rightly so when we visualise any atrocity done on any woman. Especially so, because the whole woman race is the producer of mankind. Let us imagine a community without any woman. That community will never procreate, it would become smaller and smaller and die out.

So woman is the only producer of mankind, and as we think of woman as a mother, any woman of any country, of any religion, caste or creed or status, our heads have to bow down with respect, because of the love, care, sympathy understanding, and all deep feelings that a mother entertains for her offspring, would tantamount to a unique emotional interaction between two human beings.

For a mother, the child is never big enough for showering of affection. Whether the child is big, small, grown-up or aged, the mother's love flows to him with equal intensity. Is it not our duty to place our mother above everything else in our worldly consideration?

The mother may not ask much from her son or daughter or even she may ask nothing from her grown up children, but in the rule of nature it is but natural that we, sons, owe allegiance and show respect to her, as long as we live.

Mother, sister, wife, and daughter, these are the four faces, four images of a woman, and for us, men, these are the most precious images. If any of us destroys any of these images, or distorts any of these, then we should not be called human beings, but animals, nay, worse than animals, because even animals have some code of conduct.

Ladies and Gentlemen, I do not wish to go into details over the wonderful attributes and qualities of a woman. Woman has made sacrifices for man, as history and legends would show, with no concern for herself and with all the protection she can muster, to save some man.

A woman's sensitivity would by all means revolve round love for her beloved. In this feeling or relationship with man, with her beloved, she has practically very little thought for physical involvement except for the close intimacy with the person she loves, as well as to deliver maximum joy to her beloved.

I am sorry for this long prelude to build up the vision of women among men. If a woman, a weaker sex, with higher feelings and the capacity to adorn this world with beauty and everything converted with beauty, is ill-treated and violated, there is no deeper shame for mankind. It is a shame for all of us, notwithstanding the fact that some incongruous male persons may be the violator.

The sin against a woman committed by any male member of the human race, is a slur on the whole of the male members, because inspite of their boasts and muscles, their authority and power, they have proved to be a failure to protect a woman, to offer to her proper security, while talking of the grand security of the nation as a whole.

It is true that the root of this malady, the crime against woman lies in the crooked psychology of the concerned criminal. To straighten out such a criminal's crooked mind, is not the subject of our discussion today, and we may leave that problem to social workers, medical practitioners and state authorities.

However, what is of significance to us is that if reason does not prevail, if culture, understanding, training and judgement fail, then we have only one course left to us. Fear therapy should be made operative. This fear can be evoked through stringent punishments.

The criminals who go scot free and cannot be apprehended, are of course out of our purview, but those who are caught, and whose guilt is proved, should be given the severest punishment.

I also do not wish to suggest the nature of the punishment that should be met out to the guilty person. But, suffice it to say, that the punishment should be sufficient to deter a person, to make him think twice before the embarks on a heinous career of this type.

'Eye for an eye', 'tooth for a tooth', had been the normal punishments in the good old days. In our present day, a similar schedule of punishment could be drawn up. Thus if a person knows, that he may lose a limb or his vital parts as the consequences of his evil deed against a woman, then his conscience may be forced to act automatically to stop him from any such irrational action.

Another point that naturally raises its head in such sombre and degrading situation, is that a woman who has been through the traumatic experience of a crime against her, should receive the highest acclaim from society. She should be the recipient of some award like the 'bravery award' etc. and should be at the centre of respect and reverence, instead of humiliation and antipathy. If we can mobilise enough of public opinion, then our society would come to regard such women as martyrs.

Thank you.

3
National Students Union
(Speech of the Student Leader)

Mr. Chairman Sir, our respected and honourable Minister (name and portfolio of the Minister), Respected Guests, and Friends!

This annual event of students unions of all institutions, of the country, is a memorable occasion. It is more an academical ceremony that brings us, students, from different parts of the country on a single platform, from where all student participants who wish can speak out their troubles and tribulations, their targets and achievements and their ambitions and aspirations.

Friends, may I tell you, and I know, I need not stress on the fact, youth is the period of action, and therefore, it is incumbent on us we, the students of this country, to talk less and work more. Before us lies the vast volume of work. We have to forge unity in the midst of our diversities of ways, habits, customs, traditions etc. Secondly, each of us, in his/her own way should try to mobilize student power, to act for the betterment of our country so that the basis of nationality becomes firmly rooted in our minds.

Youth is an impressionable age it is also the age for work and progress. In all our diversions, we should not forget our priority, and our priority is to advance ourselves in learning. Our parents, guardians and well-wishers are waiting with bated breath, to see us come out successful, and if and when we do so, when we fulfil their expectations, then we fulfil our primary mission.

My message to you, all my fellow students, is that on no account should we forget our goal of acquiring learning and acknowledge because that is the objective for which those who are sponsoring us, are withstanding sacrifices. It is their dream that we prove ourselves worthy of their ideal, and establish in life as responsible citizens.

When we think of this noble ideal of our parents and ideals and their simple aims of seeing us settled in life, then it should pain us to see their ambition demolished through our frolicsome and careless ways. We should take the vow therefore, on this day, that, come what may, we would not veer from our objective and spend all efforts to crown us with glory in our student period.

All work and no play, makes Jack a dull boy. This is also an ongoing adage. We have to be conscious about the world around us. We cannot and should not keep our eyes shut to our surroundings, to the happenings, the laws, the people, our people. We are the privileged ones, we are receiving education which many boys and girls of our age, of our land, are being deprived of. Therefore, it is also our duty and one of the main responsibilities that we understand our country and our people, we distinguish and mark out their needs, their anguishes, so that when we get the chance, it we do so, in later life, we would try to eliminate the negative factors, we would fight to ward off the common miseries and lead ourselves and our countrymen towards a more peaceful existence.

However, that is for the future, our plan, our programme in life, when we do get the opportunity to guide the destiny of our nation. But, before that there is the whole lot of tasks which we can attend to, without neglecting our studies or being careless to our primary goals.

We must use our spare-time in selfless work for our country. Much social work is to be done to help and educate the common populace who should be in need of the same. Sanitation, environment cleaning, adult education, even assistance in natural calamities, like flood etc. should be taken up by the student community on a voluntary basis. We can go into the villages and tell and educate villagers about the modern and scientific way of living which will make their life free from disease and disaster.

We can get ourselves acquainted with current politics, economics, and scientific and technological developments. Knowledge in these spheres would supplement our theoretical learning, and prepare the base for our future career.

Apart from these, a student should take interest and participate in games and sports. These extra-curricular activities are an integral part of our lives, just as important are improvements in our cultural and artistic sides, like dramatics, music, debates, and other institutional activities which would free our minds from the pressure of studies, and enrich our mental capacities.

Involvement in all these activities, however, is to be on a balanced scale. We should never step off from the middle path that would lead us to our educational achievements. We are never to be indifferent to our country's civilisation and progress. Along with our own studies, we should study the pros and cons of our existing system and should be aware of plugging in the loopholes, if any.

Dear fellow students, what I wish to speak out to you, would never be complete without mentioning the negative and unproductive sides of our activities. Laziness, lack of the spirit of competition, addiction to anything, idle gossiping, unnecessary pride, etc. are the minus points in the students life, according to the old Sanskrit texts. These guidelines we are to remember, and make effective in life.

Thank you.

4

Lawyers' Convention
(Speech of the Chief Guest)

Mr. President, Ladies and Gentlemen !

It gives, me immense pleasure to speak to you today at this Convention. We all are aware that practising of law is regarded as a learned profession. I need not tell this important audience here that the lawyer's is a very dedicated and committed life. The selfless service that a lawyer gives to society and his country, may or may not be compensated by the consideration that he gets in return, but the qualitative aspect of a lawyer's work, should invite great appreciation from all quarters.

The lawyer is a very important member of the community. He stands between the law and the people, as well as between the law and the authorities. He is there amongst us for the interpretation of the law of the land.

Without the lawyer, the whole legal system, the gamut of rules and regulations and official acts and decrees, would remain lop-sided or one-sided. It is also quite possible that in the urge and zeal to implement the tenets of codified regulations, there could be indiscriminate and unrestricted application of rules.

The lawyers act as a break and could provide yeomen's service to the people and to the country by the exposition of the rules and how far these are to be made effective on the violators.

Every person who is accused of an offence may not be actually guilty unless his guilt is proved in a court of law. It is the lawyer who is to assist the judge to arrive at the right decision as to whether an offence or crime has been actually committed or not.

In the lawyer's hands therefore, lies the sequence of democracy because when two lawyers successfully argue the case, for and against, from the positive and negative sides, then a greater clarification of the issue or the dispute comes to light, and the judge and the jury may arrive at the truth behind the apparently wrong action.

Therefore, if democracy in a country is to survive, if the rights of the individuals are to be upheld, the rightful participation of lawyers in the legal system is essential. It is the duty of lawyers to explain to the judiciary and to the people the various details, degrees and nuances of the codified law.

The lawyers also do a good service to the people and to the Government by finding out the flaws, the loopholes, if any, in their efforts to save their clients. It is through their arguments that the government might realise and find out the chinks and way-outs in an Act of the state, which would have to be plugged or cemented. This, the government could very well do through subsequent amendments of the concerned Act. Thus, from the point of security and general well-being, the services of the lawyers in a State are commendable.

My only submission to you gentlemen, is that, considering the great trust and responsibility reposed in lawyers, the great social service the lawyers could render to society, and the much-needed academical interest that they could bring to the legal system as a whole, the state and the community, should have much respect for lawyers.

However, no light is without darkness, no goodness is away from the touch of evil, no rightful action is rightful without wrongful inclination, and so on. This is only to indicate that since the lawyers are deeply involved in the legal ways, explanations, etc. they could have in their hands the power of reflecting the laws, and hence, it is required of them to continue strictly with their business norms.

It was Gandhiji who while practising as a lawyer in South Africa, a long time ago, discovered the true function of a lawyer. A lawyer, according to the Great Mahatma, should try to bring the two rival parties in a case, to reconcile with each other. This way, much unnecessary expenses and wastage of time could be saved.

The real lawyer would fight a case more as a challenge to the academical interpretation of the law. Further, he would be more concerned about guarding the interests of his clients against all odds. The clients come to a lawyer, sometimes, in a state of utter desperation, and in his frustrated and helpless condition, his lawyer is his only beacon light. I hope all members of the legal profession would remember this fact in dealing with their clients.

Thank you.

5
Science and Development

Mr. Chairman, Honourable Chief Guest, Ladies and Gentlemen !

We live in an age of progress. In this age one who does not develop, will stay behind and will recede. One who adopts to new means of advancement will go ahead.

In this race for going forward, modern technology is the most useful tool, which we should use to make our forward journey smooth and impressive. Technology however, has the tendency of getting obsolete. The gadget or equipment that is new today may become old tomorrow.

To protect us from such a pitfall, we have to adopt and adjust ourselves, with new technology. Each new technology is expected to improve efficiency, reduce cost and save operational time and energy, among others.

But, Science supplies us the means. We have to harness this means to our respective usefulness. To make this effective, that is, to apply scientific methods properly in our lives to make our progress more successful, we must have more and more research and development (R & D) organisation. R & D is an integral part now of our industrial network. Many capable industries are having their own research and development sectors that work for their own improvement in cost and quality.

Thus, science and technology have to run side by side. Theoretically speaking, sciences is the vast domain of knowledge, of nature's mysteries which would never exhaust, and which man can forever explore to find new methods of better living.

New theories could be invented, new formulas drawn up, new medicines, new sources of energy, production, transportation, communication etc. could lead man to enjoy and lead life, in a better manner.

Technology could be bettered through research and through improvements, on the on-going processes. As technology is made superior, efficiency increases, and the quality and standard of life become superior.

Science and technology are supplementary things. Scientific inventions and innovations are necessary for the advancement of technology. At the same time, as the need for higher and sophisticated technology is felt, man engages himself more and more to scientific inventions which would give newer bases for superior technology. Technology demand, therefore, is one of the motivations behind scientific research.

In the modern age, progress has become the pastime, so much so, that old models of cars, machinery and equipment are being discarded like old clothes. In consumer durables and goods like television sets musical systems, communication modes, refrigerators, electronic goods, etc. the world is moving so fast that there is no time to stand and ponder.

Scientists, designers and manufacturers, in fact, everybody connected with the consumer products, is on a mad race to reach the goal of maximum efficiency first. Scientific knowledge and development, are now equal partners. Science has become the mainstay of our existence.

In this set-up we can guide our children towards the scientific bend, if we have a system that puts science into their minds from an early age. Computer education, machine drawing biology and botany in their simpler forms should be included in children's curricula. We must remember, we have to keep pace with progress.

Thank you.

6
Business Meeting

Mr. Chairman, the Honourable Chief Guest, Ladies and Gentlemen !

We have assembled here to take very important decisions on quite a few vital issues. There is no doubt that when a person or a group starts a business, it (business) may be begun in isolation.

Soon however, the complex nature of the business world catches up with the solitary working of the business unit and this unit has to face competition, national and global, and also, regulations, strictures and a host of situations some of which could be favourable and some, unfavourable.

At the very outset we must realise that an industrial or business venture is not simply an individual or sectional affair, but it is a national and global affair, and hence, a venture of this kind, requires the cooperation of all, the people, the government as well as the foreigners. The foreigners are also benefited from a successful national expertise because they can also have the chance to utilize transfer of technology from both sides.

A business enterprise has to thrive on the basis of community welfare. Whether we produce goods or services the quality of our production should be the best, that is our maximum capability. Not only that, this venture should also aim at maximum public welfare.

Gentlemen, we cannot reap and keep our profits like that of a run-away fugitive. We have to live and work in society, we have to produce utility, we have to disburse that utility in an equitable manner among our fellow citizens.

Our norm should be always high, our target should be benevolent, and our working should be above board, above any question of integrity. There is no 'touch and go' in business. The business has to build up goodwill, prove its performance, sincerity and steadiness.

There are two sides of a coin. Just as we are committed to our business, we have to be dedicated towards our objectives, so also, the country and the Government have to cooperate with us, to boost us and push us in both national and international business worlds.

We do no want that the Government should help us blindly because we are national units, but some sort of security cover is required against those who seek to destroy our growth through unscrupulous acts.

Also, we must depend on our own people, our own nation to stand by us and promote and patronise our products and services, if we are able to satisfy their consumer tastes.

This love for one's own country' goods, may also be termed as true nationalism which every businessman can expect from and bank on his countrymen. when there is an irrational craze for foreign goods, and total rejection of anything produced nationally, irrespective of its quality and utility, then we businessmen are at a loss to fight a proclivity which is nothing but sort of an addiction.

We, thus, expect that our countrymen, our own people, will back us and help us to launch our own business activities. At the same time, we are entitled to hope that our Government would extend their cooperation to make our business, our venture, stand against national and foreign competition.

National competition we should not fear, if that competition is carried on in free and fair terms. About international competition also, the same contentions hold good. But, if that competition is made unfare through protective duties abroad, or unwilly exports from abroad at unreasonable price-cuts, known as 'dumping', then we should expect our Government to assist us through duty exemptions etc. We should be allowed to thrive to strengthen national life.

Thank you.

7

National Seminar on Teachers
(Chairman's Speech)

Honourable Chief Guest, Ladies and Gentlemen !

This is a big moment for me because I am addressing you, teachers, whom I regard as the most important members of our community. From my childhood, I have always maintained a deep respect for teachers.

Teachers are the builders of our society and you may say, our civilisation. The students of today will build up and propagate the civilisation of tomorrow. Once a film actress was asked the question as to what she thought about teachers, and she replied that she considered teachers to be the most perfect of beings. She was in a way right, because the students who are being taught think his teacher as the be-all and end-all of superiority.

I may tell you another small episode which is relevant in this context.

I knew the head of our coaching institute who used to get lots of school drop-outs and rowdy students of low intellectual levels, who took coaching from this institute to appear as private candidates in school-final examinations. Before selecting a teacher, he would provisionally put a teacher in the most indisciplined class. If the teacher could manage that class, could keep the class quiet, then he was in, he required no other recommendations.

I think I would tell all you teachers to keep this in mind that if a teacher is good in his or her field of teaching and if this teacher loves the students, and is committed to teach them, then that teacher would be doing his duty in the best manner. As teachers, I think we must remember one thing, and that is, that the students are not our competitors, they are our wards. There is no good student or bad student, but just 'student' who of course has his or her limitation of intelligence, his capacity of take-in and reproduce, that is all.

Parents and teachers are the two pillars of a child's citadel. The structure of the child's life and career does rest on these two pillars, and if the parents on the one hand and the teachers on the other guide, the child in the right direction, then there is every certainty that the children, all children would bloom to the best according to their inherent calibre.

Ladies and Gentlemen, teaching is one of the noblest of professions, and a sacrificing one too. It is sacrificing because the students learn not only from the words of the teachers, but also from the life and mode of conduct of the teacher. Teaching is a very responsible job. I wish all teachers everywhere will realise their responsibilities.

Thank you.

8

Political Party's Annual Conference (Govt. Party)
(Speech by a Party Speaker)

Mr. President, Honourable Guests, Party colleagues!

We have gathered here at a point of time which should be important because General Elections are round the corner. This, therefore, is an opportunity for as to review our performances and deliberate on our prospects.

Since the last general election, much water has flowed and many of the opposition parties have done better at the polls in State Assembly elections.

The results in more States were expected because our Party Leaders were more concerned about external matters like security as well as precaution against terrorism and communal dissentions within the country. However, our efforts at national integration continued unabated and our National Human Rights Commission has been doing a meritorious job since its inception only a few years ago.

Our external policies and political and economic administrations have been very satisfactory. The democratic process has been established beyond doubt, and the management of our economy has been lauded even by foreign governments and institutions.

While everything appears to be going on well and as per schedule, we have faced reversals at Assembly elections in the States. We have now analysed the causes and have come to the conclusion that such reverses are but the natural fall-outs of people's inclinations and desires for a change, for some change, which they imagine would better their material existence.

I may term this liking of our people as imaginary because economically and politically our steps have been correct. We have achieved maximum results in all sectors. Our granaries are full, our exports are booming, foreign investors and businessmen are having better confidence in our system and our native companies are spreading out in other counter countries to get firmer footholds.

Internally, the middle class population is having a much better status and the wages of labourers are increasing. But our political personalities are engaged more in other pressing preoccupations, and therefore, they have had less leisure to establish, renew and strengthen their contacts and interactions with the common people who may have nowhere to take their grievance to, except to anybody who could lend them ears, who have enough pastime for fomenting their complaints and grievances.

However, we should never regard this as idle work because our base is in the people who have voted us to power, and we have every hope that judging the results of our actions, our people will be on our side inspite of any propaganda or publicity against us.

It is, however, time now that we should, every one of our partymen, find time to be with the people to explain to them, that real progress does not consist in populist measures like giving them subsidies, pensions, free food and lodging etc. but to place the country's working on such a footing that each citizen, each individual, finds the chance to earn enough to meet his needs. We have to convince the people that aiding them with subsidies and concessions, could be regarded as a wrong principle of assisting people. The real assistance is to make the people self-reliant and self-sufficient, so that they earn more and more and contribute to the country's development, in a much bigger way.

Thank you.

9
Conference on Human Rights
(Speech of a Delegate)

Mr. Chairman, Your Excellencies, Fellow Delegates, Ladies and Gentlemen !

Man has risen to be the supreme being among all other kinds of living things. Man has achieved this height through the application of his rationality. Other qualities and attributes that have helped man to move ahead of other animals, are his spirit of cooperation and coexistence.

However, the towering ambition of man keeps on moving upward, and in its flying-high spree, he is apt to be blind to the needs and necessities of all around him. He experiences only the urge to reach his goal, to have more and more acquirements.

We may be all ambitious to a degree, because ambition also has its good points, and without ambition, at last some purpose in life, a man would be like a ship without a rudder. But, as human beings, our feelings and understanding are our main assets. If in the course of our onward rush for success, we forget these noble qualities of ours, if we be immune to and insensible towards the welfare and well being of others, who are our fellowmen, then we would definitely do injustice to others, we would commit the crime of trampling on the rights of others.

While we have every right to think of better prospects for us, we have no right to violate others' rights and requirements. How beautiful and more humane this world of ours would have been, if we did not have to hold a conference like this on human rights. Human rights would have been automatically respected and preserved. No deliberations would have been needed for its maintenance.

However, it is sad for us, human beings, that such a conference has been found to be necessary to uphold individual rights. It is sad because we are selfish enough to overlook the safety and safeguards of others from physical and mental angles. Physical hardships or tortures are unbearable enough, but no less pinching and pungent, are mental miseries and agonies.

From another side, a conference of this nature and style, shows to us that we have not lost our balance, in the zeal of our own improvement, that we are still sane enough to distinguish between the privileged and non-privileged, the so-called haves and have-nots. It may be regarded as an achievement for us, human beings, that we have not forgotten our fellow human brethren, and that we assemble from time to time, as we have assembled today, to survey the whole range of rights that all our fellow citizens are entitled to, but are deprived of.

We have now National and International Human Rights Commissions who look after and supervise on the rights of all mankind, in the national and international perspectives.

There are refugees who have been compelled to leave their homes and under militant and terrorist activities. There might be persons who are persecuted in their own countries and seek asylum or protection in another country. Their might be minorities in one country, not treated at par with the mainstream of the population. Though our deliberations might not legally achieve much yet in all countries, public opinion is a strong force, and when truth of bad happenings is not suppressed, but is allowed to come out, then our mission is achieved. That the Governments of the world have lent their allegiance to our organisation or organisations, prove the goodwill of all nations, and also show to us that hope and human happiness can still thrive in a world burdened with controversies.

Thank you.

10

Environment and Mankind
(Speech of an International Personality)

Ladies and Gentlemen !

I would like to thank, first of all, the sponsors of this meeting under whose aegis I have been able to face you and interact with you. Environment today is not an isolated subject that can be discussed and studied as something of academic interest, but environment is very much a live issue, that is intimately woven into the fabric of human existence.

To start with, we have to go back at the start of history to identify environment with nature as well as the habits and living of human and other beings. There is the environment of the cold countries and the environment of the hot and humid atmosphere. There is the environment of the sea-side, the environment of the mountains, and of the desert region.

We have also the forests, the watersheds, the greenery and so on. We may fell the woods for logs to be sold, we may reclaim the waterways for building homes, and blast the mountains to expand our urban civilisation, but we might not realise that these actions are hazardous for us, for human welfare.

When we chop off trees and bare the mountain slopes off greenery, we cut off a part of nature that was installed to supply man with the nourishment of purer atmosphere. The chimney smoke from our factories, and the chemical wastes pouring into our rivers, pollute the air we breathe and the water we drink. Further, the fish and other watery products that could provide nourishment to sections of mankind become tainted through water-pollution and may become unfit for consumption.

Thus, man is proving to be man's own enemy, by destroying nature and polluting the very surroundings where man lives. In urban areas, in cities and towns population is increasing, provision for sanitation is diminishing and the excess of transportation is getting out petrol and exhaust air into the natural environment. Many of man's maladies could be avoided, if he could breathe free and fresh air throughout the day.

We can hold meetings and discuss about protecting nature, but the task is not easy. Unless the people cooperate with the Authorities, unless the protecting and safety rules enacted by the Government were supplemented by people's coordination and self-restraint, there could be sneaking violations of rules, as also encroachments and trespassing without control.

Environment preservation is sometimes a high sounding word and at other times it becomes a way of life with the people. When children are taught from their tender age that maintaining of the natural scenery is an important aspect of living. It is a useful duty of all men, women and children to enrich nature and the natural environment by their daily acts, by keeping their surroundings and their habitation clean and healthy. It is not through regulations but through realisation that man and nature can exist in absolute peace.

Thank you.

11

Banking Development
(Speech of an Official)

Mr. Chairman, respected Chief Guest, Ladies and Gentlemen !

Banking is the main artery of our commercial life. However, as our civilisation advances, and our people become more uptodate in modern living, banking becomes a part and parcel of our lives.

In the most developed countries the banking system has advanced so well among the people, that even cheque payments are accepted in the simplest of the day-to-day cash transactions like grocery purchases etc.

The expansion of the banking system among the people especially the rural population, should be regarded as a big achievement. Not only do the extension and acceptance of the banking habits, prove to be favourable for the banking business, but also more transaction with banks will keep the people in contact with the banks. These contacts could ultimately make the people realise the various opportunities that the banking sector could open up for the different sections of the people.

But, as we know this is only one side of banking activities. Banks and the business sector have a different kind of relationship, on which depend the growth of the country and the banking sector as well.

Credit is a very important phenomenon in today's progressive process. The banks can have larger and larger deposits but that situation can hardly mean anything. For the banks this growing deposit is not for free, but at an interest.

Therefore, the banks must lend a major part of this deposit money to businessmen at a higher rate of interest, and the difference is of course to be regarded as the profits of the banks. But the banks can only earn these higher interests if their lending is correct and fruitful.

If the banks can assist and back industries and business ventures which are profitable and are capable of yielding good returns, then the banks can go on having their higher interests, while the business units backed by them may also prosper.

Sometimes, a bank has to select business activities for credit, which (businesses) which may be starting at the scratch but the nature of the business has prospects, and also the few transactions already completed, give promise of development.

It is true that the bank that is forwarding the loan, has to take risks, but then 'risk' is the watch-word of the business world. Besides, in the shrewdness of selecting good and prospective ventures, the bank Authority's correct intuition and knowledge, would play a great part.

The banker by his right decision can thus earn profits for his banking organisation, as well as he can give the necessary prop to the business venture. If the businessman and his business are genuine and if the bank can assist him at the time of teething or initial troubles when his goodwill was not built up then the bank would be really doing a great service to the nation and to national economy by helping the businessman get over his troubles and sail smoothly in the business world.

Development of banking would therefore depend mainly on two things, on the bank-manager's correct foresight as to where to lend and where not to and secondly, he has to set his priorities rightly in the context of the national business panorama.

Just as the individual bank-branches have to be concerned with their revenues and expenditure, and with the increase of their deposits-range by expanding their respective customer-range, so also the Central Authorities of the banks have to draw up other plans and programmes for expansion of banking activities in the countries.

These plans would refer to opening up of branches in new areas and in the remote parts of the country, so that business activities could continue unabated throughout the length and breadth of the country. Banking is a boon to the financial world. Let us all share this boon.

Thank you.

12

Programme on Health
(Chief of Health Association's Speech)

Mr. Chairman, Honourable Chief Guest, Ladies and Gentlemen!

I shall not go back to the common saying 'health is wealth', but I would like to ask you that you may have lots of money, but if you are in ill-health, mental depression and are physically unable to enjoy life what good is that wealth to you? You may have a rich and tasty food on your table before you, but if you do not have appetite or the power of digestion, then that food would be useless to you.

It is your duty to chalk out the best health programme for the people. We have to catch them young, the proverb goes, so, we have to make the Health Programme most effective for the children. If we can make our children strong, and can make them grow to their fullest, then they would be having a good start in life. They could then face life with a bigger confidence and in a much better shape to stand against and defeat the competitions of life.

Our programme on health, therefore, should begin with children at school and at home. There could be many affluent homes which might be careless about a child's health requirements. The balanced diet is essential for the children, so that they get and absorb the proper amount of calories from their food.

Whatever, may be the food habits of the family, the children should take in the right quantity of proteins, vitamins etc. from their food, if the parents are aware of the health value of the different food items.

Food is good for sustaining life, but the intake of the right quantity of food at different meals, is very important. The tiger is a meat eater. You may give it bucketfuls of meat, but it will eat the quantity that is just needed for one meal. It is sad to say, this instinct or restraint in consuming food may not be found in most of the human beings. If a person knows when to stop, though he may have a spread of the best dishes before him, then most of his health problems would disappear. The animals use their instinct but unfortunately men, and excuse me, even women, behave irrationally when consuming food is concerned.

Coming back to children, the all-round physical development of the child is necessary. Body-development is connected with mental progress, and equal attention at home and school should be given for the development of these two vital sides of the child.

Certainly, this parent-school attention has to be tempered and coordinated by the State Authorities. The vaccines, the injections, the administration of pills and potions at proper times and ages of a child by the school authorities and by the parents, are to be arranged. This was the child would grow up disease-free. The atmosphere in school and at home should be clean, with proper care for sanitation and healthcare. Not only the children, but also every member of the family would lead a normal and healthy life.

But, a proper health programme of the Government is to include every citizen. Health education and clean living are essential necessities for the people. The government can and must open treatment and information camps at different parts of the city so that the population is aware of the civic duties, health check-ups, etc. and of the fact that prevention is better than cure. With this, ladies and gentlemen, I would like to conclude. I would now leave it to you to make your lives more comfortable and more prosperous.

Thank you.

13
Economic Planning
(Speech of the Chairman)

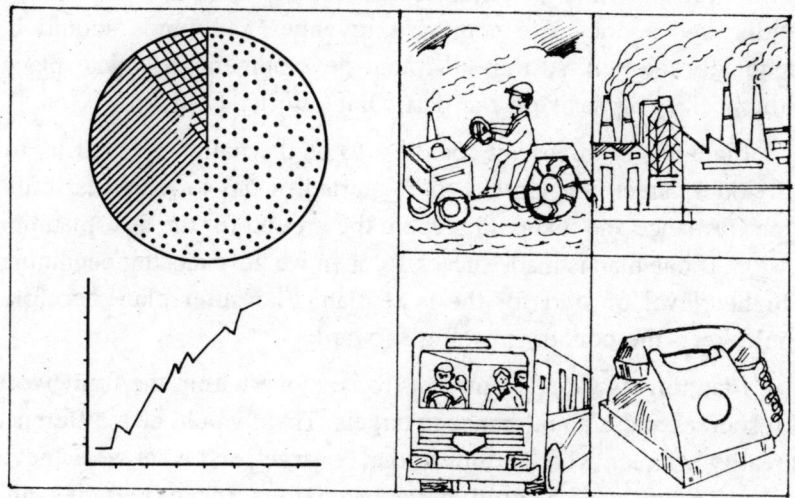

Honourable Guests, Ladies and Gentlemen !

Planning is an important word, it is also a very simple word. Let us suppose, getting up in the morning a man finds that he has to do so many things in that single day. Naturally, he would be worried with the whole burden of the work load. Where is he to begin with and where is he to end ?

Such a man should calmly draw out his priorities. The most important work is to be done first, then the work next in importance, and so on, and he would find that the pressure of the work-load is lifted from his head.

In economic planning of the state and the country, we have to follow this simple procedure. If it is education that should receive the top priority, then the Government should gear up all the work machinery for the spread of education. If agricultural or industrial development is more important for the country, then the main efforts should be guided to the priority channel.

However, proper planning should not neglect the other sectors that are outside the priority area. All sectors in the country are to be made to grow sectors like industry, agriculture, foreign trade, financial sector, transport and communications, tourism, child and women, youths, and so on. The country's revenues and funds should be adequately allotted, so that all-round development may take place, with special emphasis on the particular priority field.

Planning is important for the life of the nation as well as for individual career. A plan has to be started, it has to reach its zenith of performance and it should prepare the ground for the next planning session. If one plan is made successful then we have a better beginning, a higher level of start for the next plan. Plan after plan therefore, would keep the country pushing forward.

Planning as we all know, has to be alone within the framework of resources and with reference to targets. There would be a difference in reality between what we aim at, that is, target, and what we achieve. So, the plan itself should have provisions for exigencies and emergencies that may occur to inflict set-backs in the plan.

There could be national calamities by way of natural events like floods, epidemics, earthquakes, drought, etc. There could also be international deterents like wars, blockades, sanctions, financial crisis etc. which could harm the external sectors of the economy like imports, exports, tourism etc.

If the plan has provisions for these contingencies, then these impediments could be faced and tackled without much hindrance to the overall progress of the country. These adverse events could be laid down as set-backs. These set-backs or reverses could delay the planning process or effects, but if the working mechanism is good, the country's economy would come back on the routine lines and the yields of the various productive areas would be good by the year-end.

The plan period is important for success. If a plan is drawn up for a very long period like 10 to 15 years, then it may be difficult to keep track between the short-term and long-term results. On the other hand, if the plan is constructed for a very short time, then also the effects might not be rightly adjusted and the links between investments and outputs may not be correctly assessed.

Countries which have benefited most from planning, it appears, go on with a flexible plan. Year by year the plan effects are calculated and fitted against the targets, and new consideration, and work-outs are made to suit the new situations.

What I would like to point out is that even if the plan is disrupted, even if it could not be brought to its desired conclusions, its expected results, even then, it is better to be guided by an economic plan of revenues and receipts against expenditure. It is very much undesirable to carry on with State's affairs without a plan.

Thank you.

14

Human Resource Development
(Speech of a Delegate at the Seminar)

Mr. Chairman, Honourable Guests and Excellencies, Ladies and Gentlemen !

In today's world we are going ahead with technological developments. Scientific and engineering know-how are big terms now, which are to be co-opted in a developing system for quick progress and uplift of the living standard.

In this context and background, we have two alternatives, that is either we leave human resources as they are and concentrate mostly on industrial development, or the second is, we motivate the growth of human resources side by side with industrial and technological progress.

In the first case where human resources are left on their own, there are improvements no doubt in these resources, but such improvements are not according to any plan, but is susceptible to individual or group efforts. The results would be that some sections of the people would be developed while the other sections would be underdeveloped.

In the second alternative, human resources are given equal attention and importance with economic development, so that both human skill and efficiency on the one hand, and industrial and other developments on the other, move forward at the same speed.

In the planning system which gives as much predominance to the development of human resources as development in other spheres, the growth-effect could be more spectacular, more effective and more disbursed among the whole populace. Further, in the balanced growth of human resources, there could be less frustrations and less fears of failures. Therefore, there should be more cooperation and assistance from the people towards the success of planning.

Where human resources are not given proper opportunities for development and fulfilment, the gap between the privileged and the non-privileged widen. This breeds discontent and dissension, and the social fabric of the nation runs the risk of getting pierced and torn to pieces the balance of society is disrupted and social evils may spread to strike at the roots of settled establishments.

Human resources are being developed in all countries. The underdogs of society, the backward classes and those who are in the pits of hopelessness. and misery, are to be brought up to the level of decency and normal living. They are to be educated and made to acquire skills, to earn their own living and be self-sufficient.

In short, not only there should be plentifulness of material goods, but also there should be developments of human standards. Under this duel advancement, there is better distribution of wealth, and there is a higher stratum of human satisfaction.

We are not concerned only with material acquirements, but also with the quality of life. The material wealth is best utilised and enjoyed when these are applied to farther the designs of culture, art, literature, and enrichment of the human mind. The developed mind would foresee an adorable and enjoyable future, and that is the schedule we should all work for.

Thank you.

15

Election Success
(Speech of the Elected Representative)

Dear Friends, Brothers and Sisters of this constituency!

Today is a happy day, a day of rejoicing for all of us, not because I have won in the election, but because right has won, truth has prevailed, and the majority of the people's support for the justice of the land has been vindicated.

Dear voters, I am speechless for your overwhelming support. I hope and do promise that I shall do my best to serve all of you for a better and happier life.

You all know that I am only one arm and the government machinery has many such arms, but I am telling you that I stand for you, I realise your difficulties and your demands, not demands really, but your requirements. I must tell you that as your elected representative, I should be your real mouthpiece before the Government, and that I must bring your hardships to the national body.

I have also a plan of lending my ear to all your complaints. If I am unable to do it myself due to other pressing work etc. which would require my attention first in the national framework, I would request you to pardon me.

However, soon I would be thinking out of a measure through which you would be able to reach me and communicate with me. All of you can come to my office any day, any time, and present your letter of complaint or whatever, to my staff. I assure you those letters would be processed and would be attended to, on a priority basis.

You know that the job of bettering administrative work lies before us, and we have to do it on a cooperative scale. If I have your support, goodwill, trust and cooperation, I am sure that we would be able to bring good results in our administrative work and to lead a much superior existence.

All I request of you at this juncture is to have faith in me, your elected candidate, your rightful representative and to be patient with me, to give me some time, to put my house in order, put up my secretariat and make it function smoothly.

After that, I would be leading your case in the Assembly and also before the Federal Government when I get the opportunity. I know that my constituency needs many civil and urban facilities like better sanitation, better water-supply, better roads, and so on, and I promise you that during my whole tenure it would be my endeavour to upgrade my constituency and uplift the masses. Once again, thank you all. Let our country prosper.

Thank you !

SECTION III
CEREMONIES

1
Marriage Anniversary
(Speech of an Invitee)

Ladies and Gentlemen !

It is with great pleasure at this fifth anniversary of Mrs. and Mr. D'souza, our very good friends, we congratulate them and wish them a long married life and eternal happiness.

All our friends will bear with me that it was a very happy occasion for us when we attended the marriage of these love-birds, when with much amusement we noticed that they had eyes for only each other and no one else. I hope my friend D'souza and Mrs. D'souza will forgive us for mentioning this, but I mentioned this on purpose to point out to you friends, that we would pray to the heavens so that all married couples may be blessed with love at their marriage.

Then, friends, we remember their first anniversary and we saw the strengthening and maturing of their love in their actions and glances, and our happiness knew no bounds. Love is the foundation of marriage, and with such a married couple as D'souzas among us, we feel ourselves to be lucky.

The married life of the D'souzas was further blessed with their first born, their darling son, and the close friends of D'souzas found contentment to see them finally settle down in family-life.

At this fifth anniversary we see them blooming out properly, spreading out the petals of married life. We wish them unhindered peace and joy in their joint-life for ever, and while praying for them to have all the material prosperity and happiness, I for one, would like to come back to them every year, on this date, with my family and friends, to say to them 'many happy returns of the day'.

2

Marriage Engagement
(Speech of a close Relative)

Ladies and Gentlemen !

Today we have been treated to a very pleasant surprise by Mr. Anthony, this surprise as we all know is the announcement that his daughter Alice is engaged to be married to David who happens to be a young architect.

As her uncle, I know that Alice is a gem of a girl who is not only beautiful but is endowed with brains, and this she has shown in all her school and university results. So, David should be a very lucky person to have Alice, this combination of beauty and brains, as his wife.

As her uncle and one of her closest relatives, I feel a great pain in my heart to see her leaving her family and relatives and launch on her journey on a new and beautiful life. We wish her all the best and I would like to congratulate brother Anthony, profusely on this occasion.

It is an occassion which for the parents is a blend of greatest joy and deepest sorrow—sorrow for the realisation that the day of parting with the daughter has come, and joy because the daughter is to be settled in life. However, as a near and dear one of the family I should say that our joy knows no bounds with the knowledge that our dear Alice would start her own family life.

The ceremony of engagement has a great importance in married life, because this is the moment when two young souls are publicly marked for each other, and the romance, the dreams and the sensitiveness of the period between engagement and marriage is to be unique, and I bless Alice and David to feel and live in this period with the best of enjoyment and expectations.

Life is easy, if we know how to face it squarely driving away useless thoughts from the mind. Alice and David are educated enough to manage their own lives, and in their new life together, if they need away goodwill and good wishes, they could have these all from all of us gathered here today. Ladies and Gentlemen, give Alice and David a big hand.

Thank you !

3
Birthday Party

Ladies and Gentlemen !

    I hope you will lend your ears for two minutes to me on this happy occasion of the 16th birthday of Tara. I wish her many happy returns of the day. As her father's friend, I have seen Tara from the day she was born, and I very well remember her first birthday, her second birthday, and all birthdays after that, till today when she has stepped into her sixteenth birthday, the sweet sixteen in a girl's life. I wish her all the happiness with which she should sail through life. Please give Tara a big hand, Ladies and Gentlemen.

    Before Tara blows out sixteen candles on her cake and cuts the cake to mark the first day in her seventeenth year, I would only like to say that Tara has excelled in various ways already in her life. Besides being a good student, she has done well in sports and games, so much so that she bagged the 'all-rounder' medal in the final year of her school.

I would therefore like to pray for her to keep up this spirit of excellence in life in both work and leisure. Tara is at the sweetest crossroad of life, and I am certain that she is able to decide on her responsibilities and pick up the right way to make her mark in life.

But, those are for days to come and Tara would be having enough time to think out the shape of her life. For today, we should forget everything and rejoice in the thought and little Tara has come of age. The spotlight is on her and we should all lend our share to make this moment immensely happy for her. Best of luck to you Tara, and may we always see you smiling like this !

4

Birthday Celebration
(A Friend's Speech)

Ladies and Gentlemen !

I wish Ali many, many happy returns of the this day in his life. Ali and I grew up from kids, and so he is an open book for me. We have been through school together and then through college and there after Ali went to University and I, to my family business.

Through all these years I have observed the fine mettle he is built with. His sturdy friendship has stood by me many a time, and it was mainly his inspiration that saw me through college, otherwise I was almost leaving college and becoming a drop out. I am indebted to him for life.

On this 21st birthday, Ali is going to wear the mantle of manhood and I am sure that he would be able to cut out for himself a good niche in life through its fair weather and foul.

I wondered at Ali's ability to do well in whatever he found himself engaged in. Whether in sports or in studies, in romance, debates or in writing for the college magazine, he was always in the front line.

On this 21st birthday of his life I wish him all the success in life that is, in his career as a teacher, administrator, whatever, as well as his family life, and I have every conviction that he will be a beloved husband and a respected father, in family relationship.

So, ladies and gentlemen, and dear friends, let us give our best to Ali on this day and join the rejoicings on this very important day in his life. Long life, happiness and prosperity to Ali, and please give him a big hand.

5
Religious Ceremony
(Christmas)

Dear friends !

At this congregation to celebrate Christmas, I should only say that on this day it is incumbent on us to remember the troubles and tortures the Great Saviour of mankind under-went to deliver the human race from evil.

If our Lord and Master could bear such deep agonies, then compared to that our own sufferings would appear negligible. But we are not to do comparisons, but to propagate the teachings of our Lord. If we could incorporate a few of the tenets, the advice and teachings of our Master, then that would tantamount to the greatest respect that we could show to Him.

Religion, as we know, is a way of life. It gives us the norm that we should follow in life, to sail through difficulties and even disasters without tension or adverse effects on our minds.

If we try to get at the aims of our lives here, on this earth, we would find that the aims of life are to be to better ourselves, to enrich and develop our minds, and if we can attain some such developments, if we acquire enough confidence in ourselves, then it is our duty and responsibility, to guide others who are for guidance, to assist others who require assistance.

On this auspicious and holy day let us pray together for the betterment of our souls, and take some vows together that each day we will do something good, some good turn to somebody, and thus little by little we would add up to our soul's maturity. Amen.

6
Diwali Celebration

Ladies and Gentlemen !

I welcome you for participation at the Diwali celebration organised by our local community. Diwali is the festival of lights and on this day we decorate our homes with light, and the flittering homes and buildings give the show of a dreamland. Yes, for one day we would love to live in this dreamland, wear new clothes, and exchange sweets and gifts with our friends and relatives.

Before we start our cultural and fireworks ceremonies, I would like to take you back to the hundreds of centuries ago when according to Indian epic legend, The Ramayana, Rama the right and truthful son of Dasratha, king of Ayodhya in North India, returns after fourteen years of banishment in the forest, in which predicament he was accompanied by his wife Sita and his loyal brother Laksmana. Rama, Sita and Laksmana, had great escapades including the tale-told battle with Ravana, king of Lanka and his powerful brother Kumbhakarna and his great warrior son Indrajit.

This illustrious King Rama came back to Ayodhya, his kingdom, to take back the throne from his other brother, Bharata, and the home-coming of Rama, Sita and Laksmana, was celebrated in the city of Ayodhya, with decoration and array of lights. This, as we now, ladies and gentlemen, is the legend behind 'Diwali'.

In many parts of India Diwali coincides with the worshippings of Goddess Lakshmi and Goddess Kaali, who destroyed and eliminated evil from the face of the earth. The light-ceremony or Diwali is, thus, considered the victory of good and virtue over evil and vice. We, from our locality are meeting here today to invoke the spirit of truth and justice, of happiness and coexistence on this earth.

We celebrate this festival with crackers, presents and exchanges of pleasantries, to usher in the air and atmosphere of gaiety and glamour and banish sorrow and frustration.

So, Ladies and Gentlemen, please participate, in our celebration to make it a community success. Long live the country !

7
Welcome Speech

Mr. Chairman, Ladies and Gentlemen !

I am happy to announce that Mr. George is taking over as our General Manager, and on this day on behalf of the whole staff of our company, we welcome him to this organisation of ours, which I am sure will run most efficiency under his control.

This is no idle imagination, ladies and gentlemen, and friends, but is the reality, because Mr. George besides his long list of qualifications of expertise, has vast experience, in diverse fields, in a large span of years. It is to his credit that he was instrumental in reviving many sick industries abroad. Those units are now making profits, and are on their own legs.

Ours is a viable organisation, and as it is, we have no problems of efficiency generation. Therefore, it is our earnest expectation that he would take over our organisation to make it more and more profitable so that we, as workers and employees, could expect more considerations by way of bonus and salary-increase.

Dear friends, ladies and gentlemen, I would not like to present the impression that we are only for our own returns and gains. As staff of the company our first consideration is for our organisation because we are well aware that if the company thrives, we will all prosper, and we all know that in this interaction, Mr. George, our new General Manager would be the right person at the helm to guide our destiny to a glorious end. Friends, the only way we can discharge our obligation is to give our best to our company, and our faithful allegiance to Mr. George, and our commitment and devotion to our work and duties. On behalf of the staff, I may assure our new General Manager, all these and more from us. We extend our heartiest welcome to him.

Thank you.

8
Farewell Speech

Mr. Chairman, our respected General Managers, Department Managers, Ladies, Gentlemen and Dear Colleagues !

I rise to speak to you today with a heavy heart because today we would be bidding farewell to Mr. Simon, one of our respected and efficient colleagues. For the last thirty years, Mr. Simon has worked steadfastly, with devotion and integrity, all these years. He has been an inspiration for all of us. He has shown us that duty is to be placed before self, that work is worship, that completion of work alone gives untainted joy.

Mr. Simon has been not only a dedicated worker, but also a fine specimen of humanity and his sympathy and advice had worked miracles on many a time on our tension-ridden minds. Our younger staff has looked on him as a father-figure, and to all of us older employees, he was the universal 'brother Simon'.

However, if we keep him for longer years with us for our own solace and for getting unblemished support from him, we would not be doing justice to him, because he also needs rest and peace and enjoyment of the fruits of his labour. He also requires to lead calm, quiet and worry-free days in the evening of his life.

We are happy to announce that our retirement benefits and social security accumulations, would afford him enough returns per year to retire from the hustle and bustle of existence, and live quite a contended life.

When we bid Mr. Simon, a farewell with grief, we would like to remind you that he may be out of our working circle, but he will never be out of our minds, and whenever he likes, he may come back among us to energize us and refresh himself with our company. Let us all give Mr. Simon a big hand (Clapping).

Thank you !

9

Students' Annual Day
(Speech of the Headmaster)

Honourable Guests, Respected Parents, Teachers and Students !

Like all other years, this year also we arranged to hold your Annual students' day, and that auspicious event is today. I am happy to say, that when I look back at the year that has just ended, I feel satisfied that we have achieved quite a lot.

Academically, the name of our school has been held high by our meritorious students who were placed in the merit list of the school final examination. These students have now got admissions in prestigious colleges on scholarships from the Board of School Final Examinations of our State, and many have obtained college scholarships in the colleges in which they are admitted.

There are about ten of our students who just missed the scholarships and to them our school is giving promotional scholarships for one year, to encourage them in their studies and career.

Coming back to the activities in our own school, I find pleasure to announce that our teaching system in the school has been so upgraded that the number of failures in class examinations was practically nil and therefore, all students in all classes were promoted to the next higher classes.

In extra-curricular activities also our students have forged ahead. They have won the inter-school hockey championship and became runners-up in inter-school football tournaments. We have introduced all sorts of outdoor and indoor games, and I hope they will show their talents in the cultural programmes that they will present before you this evening, and also the play, they are going to stage as the final programme.

So, ladies and gentlemen, stay with us to encourage our students this evening, and with your active cooperation, I am certain, our students will do even better in all facets of their school-life.

Thank you.

SECTION IV
OFFICIAL OCCASIONS

1

Shareholders' Meeting
(Chairman's Speech)

Ladies and Gentlemen !

At the very outset I would like to thank you all for coming here to attend this shareholders' meeting of our company. I also thank you for your patronage of our company and your faith in our activities. I would like to he excused for my remark. It is your company, ladies and gentlemen and you have a right to know what is happening in it, what is the direction of the health of the company.

To start with, I must convince you that your company is doing quite well. There is nothing to worry about. Our production and sales are going up. It is true that competition is also catching up, but we have made adequate provisions for that. We are changing the model of our product every few months, to incorporate in it, new facilities, utilities and efficiencies. Further, we have taken up huge advertisement programmes through all the media like newspapers, radio, TV etc. We are also exploring new markets for exports, and our products are being exhibited in many expositions and trade fairs outside as well as within the country.

As a result of all these promotional and justified measures, our product has not only stood against competition, but also it is gaining good grounds in foreign countries. Hence, on the whole, the affairs of the company are well looked-after. Your company has declared 15 percent dividend this year and that is a very good performance, considering that many companies have not declared dividends at all this year.

Early next year, we would be having some rights issue and all you shareholders would have the chance of increasing your equity-holdings. I wish you all the best, ladies and gentlemen, and would expect the same trust in and concern for the company as you had shown in the past.

Thank you.

2

Board of Directors' Meeting
(Managing Director's Speech)

Mr. Chairman and Gentlemen !

We have assembled here today on a very important schedule of agenda. There are two main points which we have to decide conclusively. The first is the amalgamation of our company with our competitor company, and the second is the choice of management.

There are indicators, that our main rival company is willing to amalgamate with us. If this happens, then we would be controlling about 70 percent of the market and our separate advertisement costs as well as our competitive sales commissions would go down. We would be saving costs by that way.

Secondly, though amalgamation will be a profitable proposition for both our companies, the question of management is the main issue. We can decide by votes in Directors' meeting as to who or rather which company's official will be recommended for the top executive post in the merged company.

Alternatively, we can make it a rule that each company will have the top administrator by turn, one after the other, year by year. This would appear to be a good arrangement, the only flaw being that the change of the top executive so often might not be a better plan for the continuity of the company policies, and the management of its affairs.

Nonetheless, we must decide these issues finally today, because day after tomorrow, I would be having lunch with the managing director of the other company. The Financial Managers of both our companies would also be present.

Therefore, gentlemen tell me now what interactions I should have with my counterpart, so that after we have talked things over as the preliminary round, we may hold a joint meeting of the Boards of Directors of the two companies. That is all gentlemen, we would meet again after lunch when I could have your uniform opinion on the issues.

Thank you ! Gentlemen.

3

Another Board of Directors' Meeting
(Chairman of the Board Speaks)

Gentlemen !

I have specially convened this meeting to acquaint you with the fact that it has now become necessary to diversify our activities. Your opinion gentlemen, is necessary because we have come to a point where the demand for our product has reached saturation. All the firms in our product are having their separate markets, including ourselves. We have now reached a status of equilibrium and we cannot increase or lose our sales without disturbing this equilibrium.

It is, therefore, needed that we diversify and take up another related product the market for which is still expanding. Our research and technical departments are making a market survey on the basis of which a feasibility report would be soon made for you to decide on the issue.

Once we decide on the diversification issue, then of course, there are various other decisions to be taken, like fresh capital issue, factory expansion, accounting, advertisement and so on. However, after the product is launched in full scale, it is certain to have its market because high demand product would be chosen. Thus, we will have quite some time before we would be facing any large competition.

Hence, gentlemen, this is a meeting to inform you about the outline of our next programme. It would give you enough time to deliberate on the matter. So that when the feasibility report etc. are ready, and by the time we meet again, we may already have our opinions on the matter. Thank you once again gentlemen, for your cooperation.

4
Delegation's Visit
(Leader of the Delegation)

The Leader and Members of the host country (name of the host country) Delegation, Excellencies, Ladies and Gentlemen !

It is a great honour for me to come to your illustrious country and it gives me also much pleasure that I am leading my Delegation to your country to further economic and industrial cooperation between our two nations.

In the context of the changing world situation, it is very important to strengthen bilateral ties, because in the midst of chaos and confusion around us, these ties or bonds would remain steadfast.

Both in political and economic areas, our two countries have parted with traditional ways and values, and have instituted the new and liberalised economic systems. These have opened up vast opportunities for cooperation in-between our country and other countries.

Your country has been doing very well in the economic front. We appreciate that your country has achieved self-sufficiency in many sectors, notable among which is the agriculture and food-grains sector. Your technological development is proceeding quite fast due to a well-managed planning mechanism.

The time is now therefore, ripe and opportune to build up financial and technical collaborations, by way of joint ventures, scientific research, extension of tours, and so on. I am sure that our visit in your country would be very fruitful, and that many concrete proposals would emerge from this visit.

Thank you.

5
Welcoming Delegations
(Host Country Delegation Leader's Speech)

The respected Leader and Members of the Delegation of the foreign country (name of the country), Excellencies, Ladies and Gentlemen !

It is a great pleasure for me to welcome you to our country, and on behalf of my country, my people and my own self, I extend to you, Mr. Remos and to all members of your Delegation, a very hearty and cordial welcome to our country. It would be our sincere efforts to make your stay in our country most conducive and amenable.

As you have mentioned Mr. Leader that both our countries have lifted restrictions on trade, commerce and business venturs, it is therefore likely that our two countries can explore and work out plans for suitable collaborations in various fields, and these collaborations could be in your country, in our country and in other third countries.

You have the resources and we have the technologies. Also, the process is complementary. Your resources can be blended with our technique, while our resources can be blended with yours. The results would be beneficial to both of us.

During the stay of your Delegation in our country, we have arranged for you to see different areas in agriculture, industry and mining, and have also called up quite a number of meetings with our entrepreneurs. We hope that all these efforts from our side would produce concrete results.

Thank you.

6

Felicitation
(Speech of the Sponsor)

Mr. Chairman, Excellencies, Ladies and Gentlemen !

We are holding this meeting in honour of Dr. Amarjeet who has been acclaimed as one of the best surgeons by world bodies, and who has been admitted to the prestigious Surgery Academy of international repute.

Our country feels proud that one of our citizens has made his mark in the world forum of surgery and has pitted his skill against the best surgeons of the world.

It would be our endeavour to urge and appeal to our Government to grant him all the facilities and equipment to start his own highly sophisticated operating clinic in our country, which will not only promote and propagate Dr. Amarjeet's surgery skill, but also will help to develop his kind of superior expertise in the country.

From our organisation, we offer our humble contribution of Rs. 1,00,000/- (about US $ 3300.00) towards setting up of his clinic and fulfilment of his meritorious goal. May we cherish this hope that with his world-class skill he would stay and work in his own country and bring further laurels to his nation and his people.

I would now request Dr. Amarjeet to come up on the stage and accept the cheque and the 'citation-plaque' from the Chairman. Dr. Amarjeet, Ladies and Gentlemen, give him a big hand.

Thank you !

7
Condolence Meeting

Mr. Chairman, Ladies and Gentlemen !

I would like to inform you that a very sad responsibility has been thrust on me today. I am unable to find words to condole the death of such a devoted social worker of our state, nay of our land, as Late Mr. Fernandes.

Mr. Fernandes, Ladies and Gentlemen, has always been a good friend of mine, and I find no embarrassment in mentioning that my victory at the Local Council elections was to a great extent influenced by the fact that Fernandes was on my side.

People from all classes and strata, loved him mainly because of his simple and honest nature, his love for reality and his determination to fight against odds. If funds were not available for any free social service like adult education, health training, cleaning up of the area properly, etc., he would never get discouraged, but would set about to raise funds, for these services.

And, he did raise funds, people trusted him and had faith in his capability. We all lovingly called him 'Ferdy' even small children, and he always had that bright smile of his, for all of us. The more I speak of him, the more my heart pains. I do not know why Fate took him away from us at the ripe and young age of 32, but we will always treasure his memory, and pray to the Almighty for the eternal rest of his soul.

8
On Receipt of Award
(Speech of the Awardee)

Mr. Chairman, Authorities, Members of the Literary Academy, and Friends !

This literary award which has been conferred on me, should be the height of my glory and good luck, because this prestigious award is the coveted presentation that a writer can expect in this country.

That the Academy Authorities chose me for the award was one of the great astonishments for me. And, in return, I can only promise that in future days and years. I shall be endeavouring to better the cause and status of our literature. I would strive to bring our literature and writing to world standard and beyond.

My greatest acknowledgments, however goes to my country, its people, its habitat, flora and fauna and the wonderful variety of our thoughts and living. I have drawn my literary material from all these, and I am indebted to all these factors that shaped my thoughts. My only ambition is to stand by my country, and to enrich its culture and tradition.

I thank all of you and am really proud that I am among my countrymen. Thank you and all the best wishes for our country.

9
Inauguration of Function
(Cultural Meet)
(Speech of the Inaugurating Official)

Mr. Chairman, Excellencies, respected Guests, Ladies and Gentlemen !

It gives me immense pleasure to inaugurate the week-long cultural meeting organised by the well-known cultural organisation, International Cultural Association.

Culture is the core and kernel of human existence. It is the measuring rod of civilisation. Wealth and affluence can be had and lost in even a day, but culture requires time to grow.

The programme that start this evening and would continue for a week would cover the whole panorama of cultural activities like dance, drama, songs, small plays, music competition, picture and painting exhibition, and so on.

The main aim of holding such a function is to generate and promote cultural sensitivity among the people, especially the younger generation. A person may be a born poet or an artist, but this person has to fulfil himself in a community, he blossoms in the appreciation and encouragement of others. He still might be a writer or a painter or a singer without any-body to look at his paintings or listen to his songs. Creating art and appreciating or absorbing the same are the two sides of the coin, one side is not complete without the other.

I feel that the programmes that have been set up for you, for the people would be very satisfactory. These would give the participants enough of encouragement and provide the audience with a rich set of diversions.

Thank you.

10
Inauguration of Trade Exhibition

Mr. Chairman, Excellencies, Dear Exhibitors !

It is a very auspicious moment for me to inaugurate and open this trade exhibition and open it to the public and to the business people.

Trade is a vital artery of the economic life of a country. Moreover, we now live in an age which is approaching more and more towards globalisation, towards international commerce.

Imports and exports of goods have increased the concept of complementarity. This means, what we need the other country has, and what they require, we are producing. We can therefore interact, and the result is reciprocal. The way, we save cost and have advantages of comparative costs.

Trade exhibitions are important media through which we get to know each others' products. One speciality of this exhibition is that a special 'services' sections is set up where different countries businessmen can see what specialised services are offered by individual countries.

There will be interchanges of views and opinions and expertise, at these meets, and we are expecting many business delegations from various countries to visit this exhibition.

I hope this exhibition will serve its purpose in expanding your knowledge and that many business deals will be concluded before this exhibition ends in two-weeks' time.

Excellencies, honoured guests, ladies and gentlemen, I now declare this exhibition as inaugurated, and would request our Chief Guest, the Honourable Minister of Commerce to cut the ribbon at the entrance to open formally the exhibition.

Thank you.

11

Presiding over Annual Function of Association

Gentlemen !

First of all I would like to greet you and thank you for attending this Association meeting. Our 'Poor Relief Association' has now completed five years, and I feel pride to announce that in these years, our Association has shown a creditable performance.

When we started, our immediate aim was to give relief to poor community of our area and locality. Our next aim was to expand our relief work to our State, and by and by the whole length and breadth of our country.

We have been successful in the two stages of our mission. Our workers are now engaged at the state level and our finances are now applied to that effect. Our main objectives have been education and employment. Our Association has arranged primary schools for free education for poor children and also we have opened a training centre for women where married and unmarried women can learn various commercial arts and activities, like tailoring, cookery, food preservation, embroidery, and so on.

It gives me therefore, immense pleasure to preside over this Annual function of this Association. The secretary of the Association will later on give you the details of Association's activities and the patronage and assistance that we have been receiving from the State Government and various types of organisations. It is, however, required that there should be more publicity for our Association. One of our patrons would soon be sponsoring a charity cultural function to raise funds as well as to bring our Association to the limelight. I have every hope that by our next year's meeting, our Association would acquire nation-wide fame.

Thank you.

SECTION V
SITUATIONS

1
Picnic

Friends !

I would like to say a few words before we start properly to partake of the enjoyment of this picnic. This picnic is not the yearly official picnic that we hold where from the top executive of our office to the common personnel, participate. Since that annual picnic becomes a little too formal and thus goes, in a way, against the spirit of the picnic atmosphere, we have planned this outing.

We have arranged this mid-year picnic as an informal affair where all officers and all subordinates can participate freely and derive pleasure from mixing and exchange of thoughts and funs.

Friends, I think, you all know that there is an etiquette in picnic. Picnic-time is that period of hours when we have to forget ourselves and give ourselves up to community or friendly enjoyments. We should not hold ourselves back, we should behave freely and expect others to do so.

In that spirit of freedom of action, thought and speech, let us enjoy our day, today. That is the way we can make our picnic a success. So, friends, come one and come all, and let us fulfil ourselves in our picnicking. Welcome, and three cheers for our picnic success.

2
Banquet Toast

Mr. Simon, the Leader of the International Passenger Car Association, Excellencies, and honourable Guests. the illustrious Mr. Simon and his expert delegation has brought the message of close contact between his country and ours. Our two countries are now going to be locked in a long-standing economic and business ties. We wish Mr. Simon and his delegation a very pleasant stay in our country and a safe and satisfied return to their own. I propose a toast to the health and prosperity of the members of his delegation. I also propose a toast to the bright future of our two countries. To Mr. Simon and his Delegation, Gentlemen ! (The host raises his glass of wine along with others and drinks from the glass.)

3
Club Meeting
(Secretary's Speach)

Gentlemen !

We have been called upon to hold this extraordinary meeting of the Executive Committee of the Club to decide on a significant development on which our Club rules do not provide any provision.

It has been observed Gentlemen, that many club members are bringing their guests with them. Our food and drinks are sold at a concession, and we thought, that is, we were under the impression that members of the club would mainly bring their relatives and immediate friends and would keep the number of guests restricted, but it appears that they are not paying any attention to this on their own.

I, as the Secretary of your club am entrusted with the well-being and discipline of the club, and hence I propose that we amend the guest rule of the club and keep the guests limited to immediate relatives and to one or two in number at one time. If this meeting of the Executive Committee agrees to this amendment, then we would proceed formally to do the needful. (The Executive committee agrees). Therefore, gentlemen we call off this meeting, and would meet again for necessary action.

Thank you !

4
Welfare Society
(Chairperson's Speech)

Ladies and Gentlemen !

Our welfare society is for the uplift of pressurised and pressed women. The rights of women are established all right, but could not be properly implemented. The reason is that the meekness of the women and their social upbringing, keep them quiet and prevent them to come out in the open to denounce their tormentor.

However, society is now moving forward. Women only can understand the misery of women. As women's association, we have therefore taken up the cudgel to strike at the roots of social evil, social exploitation. In this struggle against the misdoings against women, we purport to educate women and make them independent because one of the causes of the upperhand wielded by those who mistreat women, is women's dependence on others.

Secondly, we would like to have as much cooperation from the people as possible. If public opinion is adequately built up, then those persons who exploit the women, would lose moral support and would be weakening from inside.

At this meeting therefore, we would enroll volunteers, both male and female, who would be keeping tags on injustice to women, in their area and elsewhere, and report the matter to us. We would seek to rectify the wrongs by peaceful means, but if that fails, we would not back out from taking stricter and stronger steps against the evil doer or evil doers, because the law is with us.

In most of the cases of ill-treatment of women, vigilance and good advice are enough to bring the culprits back to their senses. It is thus, our motto to avoid all forms of confrontations, and pursue pacifying means to maintain peace.

Thank you.

5

Get-together
(The Host's Speech)

Ladies and Gentlemen !

I am very happy to have you all here. We do not get the chance to meet often, all of us, like this, at one place and at one time. We have our work, our preoccupations, and yet we do meet sometime, we need to relax, to get to know about each other.

It is mainly with this aim that I have invited you today, you who are our like-minded friends, who will not criticise or complain, but will accept us and others, as we are.

I think, it is good to meet sometimes to refresh ourselves with small and big talks, and laugh away our cares with the help of others who are dear to us. I hope you will enjoy this get-together, and that tomorrow will give us new energy to face the future. Thank you friends, and enjoy yourself.

6

Cocktail Speech
(Guest's Speech)

Friends, Ladies and Gentlemen !

I would like to thank our host for calling us at this cocktail on such a fine evening. As we sit together and talk and as the wine and liquor get into us, we are sure to feel happy, and we thank our host a second time to provide us with this prospect of pleasure.

In this small gathering as we sip our drinks, many of the loads are lifted from our chests, and we return homes in a light-hearted mood. I hope we will add our respective shares to build up this mood. Thank you all.

7

After Dinner Speech Of The Host

Ladies and Gentlemen !

This dinner is the last of our engagements, in the deliberations and interactions between our two business delegations. For the last three days we have had a tight schedule of meetings and visits, and I am sure that both our sides are now satisfied with the talks and deliberations.

I am thankful to the Leader of the Visiting Delegation who has given us firm assurances that we may expect another business Delegation from their country at the end of this year, counterparts in our country.

We would be very happy to entertain such a Delegation and we hope this would mark the beginning of reciprocal visits into each other's country. We are looking forward to such prospects, for which we extend our heartiest thanks. With this, I bid you farewell and wish happy journeys to all of you.

8

Post-Dinner Speech of The Guest

Ladies and Gentlemen !

First of all I extend our thanks, to the host-country for the wonderful welcome and hospitality that we have received here. Our programme and schedule was very judiciously drawn up, keeping in view the different sectors of economic and business activities that we represent in our Delegation.

We have been able to meet with our counterparts in your business fields with similarity of interests, and I am sure that after both our sides discuss the opportunities in our respective countries, we would be able to finalize a number of deals.

As leader of my Delegation, I would like to extend an invitation to your business community representatives, and especially to you who is the leader of your Delegation, personally. I would only like to add that our mission in your country has been very satisfactory for which we are thankful to your Authorities and to you all.

Thank you.

SECTION VI
MISCELLANEOUS

1
Children's Society
(Secretary's Speech)

Mr. Chairman, Ladies and Gentlemen !

I am glad to point out to you that our society which has been catering for development of children has been continuing and thriving on the cooperation from you, the parents and the public.

Our main objectives have been to bring up a child in all its various dimensions. Childhood is the most impressionable age. It (Childhood) has the ingredients of a soft clay which can be moulded in any way. It should be the duty of parents and the society as a whole, to create the favourable atmosphere which would draw out the special talents, the particular inclinations and tendencies of a child and magnify these to their fullest extent.

Different children have different attributes. If all these attributes are cemented under a common formula of living and bringing up, then the extra-ordinary qualities of a child, if any, would be lost to the child and to the community. We are giving stress on this individualistic nature of a child's growth, because we believe, and it has been proved, that each child is different in its own way.

Our society thus tries to find out this special quality hidden or lying under the surface, in a child. We arrange for different diversions, different tests, different opportunities and outlets for the child to awaken the sleeping faculty in it (child). We strive to provide a child various set-ups wherein through the child's hobbies and interests, the child could give full reins to its wishes and aspirations.

We provide the children various kinds of toys and books, as well as materials for painting, drawing and for doing sculpture work. The children give vent to their interests through these work-plays, and the child itself as well as we, the society people, come to know the line of work and affinity which a child likes most. We make suggestions to parents and schools, regarding these tendencies.

However, ladies and gentlemen, you would realise that a target like ours could be much expanded, for which we require money, material, space etc. We would therefore, appeal to parents and Authorities to fully cooperate with us.

We have kept the children's membership fees very low to encourage large-scale participation. We have to now approach the Authorities for grant of larger space and accommodation to us, as well as we would appeal to parents with more means to contribute for our project.

With such cooperation from parents and Authorities, we are certain that our mission would proceed smoothly. The mental standard and performance-level of a child when it grows to be a man, would be much more, to add to the nation's resources.

Thank you.

2
Ladies Meeting
(President's Speech)

Honourable Guests and Ladies !

This meeting has been convened to discuss a few issues particularly related to women, that is, distressed women. It is not our intention to keep our menfolks out of our thoughts and discussions, but we have to make it purely a ladies' affair because we have a few ladies with us who would be telling you their tales of sorrow, misery and helplessness. These women who are from rural or semi-urban places as well as from poverty-stricken areas of the cities, might not be able to narrate their stories before men.

These ladies have found out and assisted by our volunteers, and brought to us by and by. One of them has been deserted by her husband after he took with him all her ornaments and valuables. The other was criminally assaulted by her employer, the third was beaten black and blue by her in-laws. There are other women also who have expressed their wishes to our volunteers to come under our wings.

But our resources are limited, and since their situations are not totally unbearable at this moment, we have advised them to continue for a while. We would take them also under our care at the opportune time.

Our main duties now are to rehabilitate these women, and find them proper work, so that the black clouds which have settled on their minds may disappear.

We have therefore, called this meeting, so that you can get somewhat acquainted with these unfortunate women, learn about them first-hand, and then help them. I would request you to explore your sources of influence and acquaintance to find proper rehabilitations for these women.

That is all for today, and thank you very much for attending this meeting.

3
Soccer Championship
(Speech by President of Football Association)

Honourable Minister of Sports and Culture, respected Guests, Ladies, and Gentlemen !

It is my great privilege to announce the beginning of the prestigious National Soccer Championship in which sixteen teams from all over the country are participating.

This championship was started ten years ago, and the venue of the championship is changed every year from one city to another. All these teams have done well in their regional spheres, and it is expected that when they clash and contest with one another at the national level, they would bring out their best to excel in the competition.

This is mainly the target of this Championship, which requires that the teams should face competition in a larger scale to draw out their maximum capacities from their inner depths.

We have distributed complimentary tickets of this Championship to various schools, colleges and sports organisations, so that our young hopefuls in games and sports, can better their own performances from the instances of the senior soccer players of the country.

So, Ladies and Gentlemen, we are certain that you will all have a good fare of soccer entertainment during the period of this championship.

Thank you.

4
On Joining as Manager of a Company

Respected Colleagues and Staff of the Company !

I have just taken over as Manager of your Company, and this is the first day of my new office. On this auspicious day, it is but natural that I would like to meet all my staff members, each one of you.

You must know that all of us have to work as part and parcel of a big machine. A big machine may have bigger parts of components, and it may also have smaller or even minute parts like nuts and screws etc. The big machine will work smoothly if all the parts are fitted well in their places. Even if a clog or a screw is out of place, the machine will not work properly and may even stop completely.

All of us are parts of our company, some big and some small parts according to their ranks and work-loads. But each one of us is important as far as the efficient working of the machine is concerned.

If any one of us drop off or fail in our duties then this whole company machine may work below par in efficiency.

My work is not to supervise and only dictate, but to think and devise ways by which the company may make profits. Unless there is more production, there are more sales, more profits, the company may lag behind others, our goodwill would fall and our share-prices might go down. So, every one thing is connected with every other thing, each step is followed by the other. In whatever position or status you may be working, it is expected that you will not neglect your duties, and keep the company going well.

This would leave me enough opportunity to frame out policies for betterment of the company as a whole. Our remunerations, bonuses, perquisites and all other considerations depend on the health of the company, and on its perfect running. I hope you will remember that, we all will remember that. And so let us all go back to our work, to our duties, to help the company earn laurels nationally and internationally.

That is all, and thank you !

5
On Taking-over as Secretary of Labour Union

Mr. Chairman, Dear Friends !

You have placed a great responsibility on my shoulders, by selecting me as the secretary of this Labour Union. But, first of all I must thank you all, dear friends, who choose me to guide you and fight for your rights. Labour and Capital are the two main factors of the production process. We are as much important to production as capital and business policy.

Labour does not want profits, it does not want fat bank balances or luxurious living style, though in very developed countries labour is much respected and enjoys a high standard of living.

What we require is to meet the necessary things, food, clothing, shelter, recreations, so that our working power is recharged, we can recoup our physical loss and exhaustion. Labour power or working energy is a worker's capital and that capital has to be preserved. Friends, it would be our duty to keep our capital, that is our labour, our working power intact. That is our moral and legal right, and we will fight to uphold that right.

However, friends, I cannot but remind you that all rights have duties attached to the same. We must perform our duties well to claim our rights. Please remember that and the rest you can leave to me. I shall leave no stone unturned to see that labour is not exploited, and that labour gets its proper share of the total national revenues. Praise be to our country, and praise be to our labour. Long live labour unity. And once again, I thank all of you.

6
On Taking-over as Association Presidentship

Mr. Chairman, Honourable Members of Traders Association, Ladies and Gentlemen !

It is a great honour that you have conferred on me today by electing me the President of the North City Traders Association. I am grateful to you, ladies and gentlemen, for the trust that you have shown in me, and I have confidence that your faith in me, will guide me to get better performances of our Association, in the current year.

I am proud to announce that in the previous year, many ladies joined our Association, they opened their shops and other business activities in our area. I would urge that more ladies with drive, skill and means, should join our Association, as they begin their business career in this part of the city.

Dear members, in the last few years our Association achieved much but there is much more, yet to be achieved. First of all, we have to take up the issue with the Authorities to allow us to keep our shops and establishments open during all festivals three or four hours after the statutory closing time. At present we are granted the extension only during the main religious festival, but there are many other auspicious and ceremony days when our prospective customers have to turn away from our closed shutters.

Secondly, we have to increase a little our membership contributions for advertising our shops and products in newspapers and television, turn by turn. Also we have to open one or two more toilets and drinking water stands in our shopping arcade.

Friends, you have put your trust in me and now I have to request for one favour from you, and that is your cooperation, without which we cannot make ours among one of the best shopping complexes in the city, and when we do that we can attract more tourists to our shops.

Assuring you of my best ability and attention towards my responsibilities. I would urge you to look at the future with radiant hopes.

Thank you.

7
Addressing A Press Conference
(Convener's Speech)

Mr. Chairman, and friends from the Press !

We have invited you to meet the Leader and members of our Delegation that would be visiting many countries to extend and expand trade and business ties between our country and other countries on bilateral basis.

Mr. Ravi who is leading our Delegation to various African and Asian countries, is a well known industrialist, having business interests in engineering goods, construction, textiles and hotels. We are sure that under his leadership, our Delegation would do very well in foreign lands. The main aim of our Delegation would be to explore the avenues through which bilateral ties may be strengthened.

It may be necessary for those foreign countries which our Delegation would visit, to send their Delegation to our country so that a proper rapport may be established and business interactions may be generated.

Ladies and Gentlemen ! you will now be provided with slips. Please write down your question, your name and the newspaper, magazine or news agency etc. that you represent. You are then to raise your hand with the slip, and your question will be brought to our table and Mr. Ravi will answer your questions.

First Question from the press — Do you have any preference for any country among those that you are visiting ?

Delegation Leader — In business, there is preference only for maximum returns within the legal framework. Hence, all countries are equal to us regarding their economic prospects.

Second Question — Is there any special sector on which you will give more stress, like industry or agriculture or mining. ?

Mr. Ravi — Though we will treat all business prospects or ventures equally, we would like to expand more in the industrial sector and the tourism sector.

Third Question — Is there any financial agreement like double taxation exemption, banking facilities, on your agenda ?

Mr. Ravi — These financial agreements are important for smooth business operations. On this visit, we will look into the existing bilateral system, with each country, and on our return we would suggest to our Government about improvements, wherever necessary.

Fourth Question — Since you will be visiting many adjacent countries, would you seek advantage in one at the cost of disadvantage in another ?

Mr. Ravi. — Advantage in one country should not be obtained at the cost of loss or disadvantage to another country, whether situated far or near, that is our objective.

Fifth Question — Your Delegation does not include representatives from important export industries like automobile, leather etc., why ?

Mr. Ravi — Ours is an exploratory mission and not technically an export-promotion one. So, established exports sectors have been kept out.

The Convener — Ladies and Gentlemen ! though we would like to continue with such an important and intelligent question-answer session, yet I am constrained to say, that there are hosts of schedules and arrangements which are to be met. So, friends ! we have to conclude this session now, and would welcome all your best wishes for the success of our Delegation abroad.

Thank you.

8
On Joining as College Principal

The outgoing Principal, Heads of Departments, Members of Staff, Ladies and Gentlemen !

On my assuming office as the Principal of this College, I, first of all, would pay my respects and my compliments to professor Madan, the outgoing Principal, on the excellent guidance and leadership that he provided to the staff and students of this college.

As your new Principal, the first principle I would like to install is discipline. Youthful outbursts and outlets of energy are acceptable, but the college authority would not stand or tolerate any indiscipline, any unruly bahaviour.

As students, you must seek your best developments your best goals and in this way you will fulfill your own dreams, as well as those of your parents and well-wishers.

Good health is the greatest wealth, and hence, apart from the college gymnasium, I would like to open a health-club attached to our college, so that students may have instruction on preservation and perpetuation of good health.

I would also like to open cultural training centers where students with cultural bent can practice music and other arts. As for academic advancements, I would have the library rules tightened so that students can go their only for reading and studying and not for idle chats etc.

College life is freer than that of the school but freedom also has its boundaries. Acquiring of knowledge is the first purpose for which you come here and you are required to fulfil that. I would like to introduce periodical examinations at which all of you have to appear.

Students are dear to a teacher, and your well-being would be my prime consideration. As your Principal, it would be my obligation to assist needy students or students who have to suddenly face financial contingencies. We would see, by all means, that the academic careers of such students are not hampered. With this, I would like to wish you all a very bright future.

9
Charity Performance
(Speech of Secretary of Organising Committee)

Mr. Chairman, Honourable Patrons and Guests, Ladies and Gentlemen !

At the very outset, I must tell you that this performance that we are going to hold today, has been possible through the active cooperation from all of you, from the public, and the untiring efforts of our volunteers and everybody connected with this performance.

The play that you would be seeing on this stage, a few minutes from now, is acted upon by famous actors and actresses without any consideration of gains. If they had not taken part, if they had not lent their names, it would have been difficult to raise funds. Therefore, our thanks and gratefulness go to them, and we wish them more and more successes in their career.

We are also grateful to our patrons who encouraged us to hold this performance when they learnt that the money was to be raised for disabled children, for their training and education, so that they may become self-reliant, as they grow up in age.

The public in general has also contributed freely, learning about the cause of the Charity. We have already had negotiations with the Authorities, to have a much bigger place including school, playground, hostel for these children.

If the Authorities can provide us with the major part of the finance, then the remaining portion of the money we can raise from such charity shows, in different cities of the country.

What therefore, we require ladies and gentlemen, is your cooperation and your goodwill, which will enable us to keep our energy, and which will provide the blessed resort and shelter for the children who are at a disadvantage.

Thank you.

10

Vote of Thanks
(Secretary of the Organising Committee's Speech)

Mr. Chairman, Honourable Guests, Respected Participants at the Seminar, Excellencies, Ladies and Gentlemen !

Our seminar on Human Rights has been a great success, if press remarks and attendance at the seminar are any indications.

For this overwhelming success. I should first of all thank the sponsors of and participants at the seminar. More so as the participants belong to eminent walks of life and they managed to stay their preoccupations to attend this seminar, and give the seminar the benefits of their erudition and experience.

Hence, our grateful thanks are directed to all members of foreign and national delegations. But we must, in the first place thank the Honourable Ministers of our Government who, inspite of their austere and important schedules were available for our inauguration and valedictory sessions.

Our thanks also go to the members of the press and other media who have correctly reflected the views and decisions of the seminar. We are thankful to our respectful audience without whom the colour and glamour of the seminar would have been absent.

Our thanks are due to all the foreign countries whose Ambassadors and Mission Heads attended the seminar.

The organising staff and every worker connected with the holding of the seminar are to have our gratitude and thanks.

Before I conclude. I therefore thank you all once again for your excellent cooperation and this seminar will remember everybody's share in its success.

Thank you.

11
Motor Rally
(Sponsor's Representative's Speech)

Ladies and Gentlemen !

This vintage car rally has a long tradition in this city where it is being held as the fifteenth such annual event.

In this Rally, we have fifty participants whose car models go back to more than fifty years back. The purpose of this kind of Rally is a simple one. It shows man's love for antique things.

Ancient things have a beauty of their own and the passenger car is no exception. Besides providing us a glimpse of the development of automobile engineering and industry over the past decades, we also witness the ingenuity with which the human mind first constructed this mode of transport.

Incidentally, we have among us a 65 year old gentleman among the participants, who has kept all along with him the first car which was gifted to him in his teens by his father.

Ladies and Gentlemen, car models have changed and improved, and car-speed has broken records, but our affection for old cars still persists. Ladies and Gentlemen, old is gold.

Thank you.

12

Fashion Parade
(Speech of President of Organising Committee)

Excellencies, Ladies and Gentlemen !

The controversy about 'Fashion Parade' is not yet over. Getting over this controversy as to whether the Fashion Parade is good or bad, we must add that a rich fare awaits you in which we will see the top models of the country displaying various garments which have been designed by a well-known foreign designer, for this summer season.

Since, the hotel auditorium is comparatively small, we had no alternative but to restrict the number of audience for any one show. But the show will continue for three days, and I think this period would be enough to include all interested visitors.

Fashion Parade in this modern age has acquired a great importance because today culture consists in a blend of actions, gestures and postures. A dress that is hung on a showroom clay model, may look and sparkle differently, when it is actually worn and displayed in walking, standing and so on. The fitting of the garment and the movements of the body within the garment, are very much necessary to find out the desirability of the dress.

I am sure, ladies and gentlemen, that you will find satisfactions about our displayed garments and that our models will perform to the best of their ability and skill.

So, ladies and gentlemen, judge and enjoy, and a very good evening to you all.

Thank you !

13
Beauty Contest
(Speech of Chairman, Organising Committee)

Mr. Chairman of the Jury of Judges, Members of the Judges, Excellencies, Honourable Guests, Ladies and Gentlemen !

I have the honour to present to you a very glamorous pageant of beautiful ladies who have placed themselves in a competition for selection as the Beauty Queen of the year, i.e., Miss World.

These young girls, will now pass before you in a parade of beauty. There are exactly fifty five beautiful ladies from all over the world. These are not ordinary girls, mind you, ladies and gentlemen, but they are the queens of their own countries, the most beautiful girls, pride of their nations, who have worn the crown of beauty queens in their respective lands. I warmly welcome all of you girls and I wish you all the best ! Ladies and gentlemen, please give them a big hand as they pass before you on the stage.

We believe these contests are very important to distinguish and find out the best beauties, who also are endowed with best brains.

The questions they answer instantly without batting their eyelashes, are much above ordinary intelligence. Also the tests they go through would at once pronounce them as extra-ordinary persons.

Ladies and Gentlemen, our contest is about to begin, and I am sure that at the end of the contest we will have before us three young Ladies, the Winner, the First Runner up and the Second Runner up, who have in them the combination of the best beauty and best brains.

Thank you.

SECTION VII
DEBATE

1
A Debate on Divorce
(Each Debator is alloted a Fixed Time Period)

A. Debator against Divorce

Mr. Chairman, Sir, (in a Debate no other person is addressed)

Before we bring in divorce, I would like to bring everybody to the wedding night, the night when two pulsating, throbbing hearts meet, at the marriage or nuptial bed when marriage is first consummated.

And before that as well, when the marriage vows were taken before the altar or the holy fire etc. All these sacred accepted ways and means of our society which bringing two young hearts together, bind them in matrimonial ties, and pronounce them, as husband and wife. I would like to place before all.

The hopes and aspirations of this young couple, their glorious aim of raising an ideal family, and to establish them as a vital and vibrant unit of society, all these and other dreams could be fulfilled, should be fulfilled, but for the dangerous legal barricade known as 'divorce'.

Any sane family man would ask himself or his better half, why this terminology exists at all, who invented it, who implemented it?

Divorce is the bane of married life. This vicious bogey had from time to time filtered into peaceful married life, had concocted and distorted the sweet and sour words of a love-life, and with the ill-will breeding so-called well-wishers, had permanently separated a husband and a wife when all, these normal souls desired was to patch up their quarrels and differences, if any, and thereafter, live happily and sleep in each other's arms.

Sir, what worse and demonic evil could be generated than by Divorce, which distroys a man, a woman, their children and their family. The family is shredded, scattered to the wind, the children, the suppliant human saplings are nipped in their buds. There are social organisations, welfare societies, but alas none has come forward to strike at the roots of Divorce norms, the greatest malady of our social and personal life.

Marriages are made in the heaven, destiny binds the marriage knot between a male and a female, and it is the thrill, the experience of the married life, the small and big adjustments, that turn so sweet at the evening of life, when the petty and periodical outbursts of temper would appear as child's play.

Should we therefore bear with such an outlandish system, I would ask any sane and sensible man, and I am sure what answer I would get, the over-whelming support of eliminating this venomous rule of law.

Mr. Chairman, Sir, I have had my say, but my voice is choked midway when I visualise the flame and the catastrophe Divorce spreads in society, and I for one will not rest in peace as long as the monstrous Divorce law persists.

B. Debator in Favour of Divorce

Mr. Chairman, Sir !

I give full credit to the speaker who spoke before me for his big words that appeared so high-sounding, but were apparently so empty inside. His is a good speech, I admit, but good only from an imaginative perspective which was bereft of any practical overtones.

The way my previous speaker depicted the trickle-toffee life of a married couple, proves that he never had any glimpse, any insight into the life of a married couple, sweet and sour to quote his exact words.

The pulsating and throbbing bride, he said, on the wedding night and the nuptial bed of his Arabian tales, these are true indeed for many a couple. But has he the knowledge, the data of many more throbbing brides whose pulsating first married nights turned into tremor-struck horror, when they found their life-partners, their revered husbands, coming to the glorious bed in a drunken state with wobbling feet and trembling hands, hands that trembled not with adulation or excitement but with incapacity and worthlessness.

If this is the beginning of a married life, which could be the stark realities for many maidens, where from would come the high hopes, the lofty ideals, the bridal aspirations.

Our friend, I am sorry to say, failed miserably to paint the married life in its true colour. It is not the question of occasional disputes, the tiffs and tussles, that may lead one partner or the other or both to become desperate enough to sever the wedlock knot.

The considerations for divorce may go much deeper into the behavioural patterns of the husband and the wife, their mental agonies, miseries and frustrations, their or women's physical torture and oppressions, their literal enslavement, insecurity and demolition of personality.

Sir, if we exclude a few criminal minded and designing women from the purview of the whole lot of the women-race, that stands as the symbol of motherhood and procreator of mankind, this woman, what could be her main aims in life ! Her aims are, as we all know, are to establish a home, to bring up her children, and to glorify her abode with grace and beauty and love.

But every person has a right to live honourably, respectably, to fulfil himself or herself, to bring out the best in him or her, to rise and shine in the midst of society.

When these prospects are mercilessly cut short by one partner, to subjugate the other, to possess the other's, body, heart and soul, when ill-treatment and humiliation are meted out to this partner he or she mostly she, when women for instance are treated no better than chattels or even animals, when living every moment turns into a curse, a living death, then there is no alternative for the state, for the society, for the well-wishers, to intervene to protect the hapless and darkened souls and extricate them from the tentacles and clutches of their persecutors. Divorce is a social saviour, a gift for the miserable, a boon for the mentally blind.

SECTION VIII
EXERCISES

1
Democracy versus Socialism

Government by representatives — peoples' participation — public opinion — socialism or state control — advantages and disadvantages.

2
Industry versus Agriculture

Industry's scene — agricultural base — importance of foodgrains and cash/commercial crops — industrial labour — agricultural worker — balanced growth of agriculture and industry.

3
Urban and Rural Life-styles

Speed and glamour — peace and quiet — more opportunities in cities — more cooperative life in villages — villages support city — food — cities provide other goods — suggestions.

4
Retiring Person's Speech

Long service — habit of work — love for work-place — retiring man's sadness at leaving — his prospects of a happy life.

5
Film Award
(Best Actress)

— Sponsor's remarks — best actress — acting skill — devotion and hard work — popularity and box-office success — bright future

OUR OTHER PUBLICATIONS

ENGLISH IMPROVEMENT

G-1	Grammer And Composition	60.00
G-2	Boost Your Vocabulary	55.00
G-5	Spelling Power Made Easy	35.00
G-7	3000 Synonyms & Antonyms	55.00
G-8	3000 Idioms & Phrases	60.00
G-9	3000 Quotations	60.00
G-10	3000 Proverbs	55.00
G-11	Common Mistakes In English	80.00
G-19	Dictionary Of Idioms & Phrases	60.00
G-25	Dictionary Of Quotations	50.00
G-26	Improve Your English	35.00
G-28	Improve Your Vocabulary	70.00
G-29	Dictionary Of Synonyms & Antonyms	110.00
G-33	Common Errors in English	70.00
G-34	Improve Your Idioms & Phrases	35.00
G-41	Basic English Grammar for Schools	35.00
G-45	Dictionary Of Proverbs	45.00
G-58	How To Write Correct English	50.00
G-66	Spoken English	30.00
G-105	How To Write Correct English	30.00

GENERAL KNOWLEDGE

G-97	Test Of Verbal Reasoning	55.00
G-78	Goodwill's Book Of General Knowledge	35.00
G-117	Goodwill's Encyclopaedia Of General Knowledge (with supplement)	220.00

BOOKS ON QUIZ

G-35	G.K. Quiz	40.00
G-51	World Facts At A Glance	40.00
G-52	Do You Know ?	35.00
G-54	India Quiz	35.00
G-56	1250 Questions & Answers : Quiz Book	35.00
G-57	Super Quiz Book	35.00
G-62	Sports Quiz	35.00

G-68	Science Quiz	35.00
G-74	Readymade Quizes (Foreign Reprint)	35.00
G-75	Standard Quiz book (Foreign Reprint)	35.00
G-123	500 Amazing Questions & Answers	60.00

BOOKS ON PUZZLES

G-86	Puzzles For High, I.Q. (Foreign Reprint)	50.00
G-87	Critical Thinking Puzzles (Foreign Reprint)	50.00
G-92	250 Challenging Puzzles	60.00
G-111	Challenging Science Puzzles	50.00

LANGUAGES SERIES

G-60	Learn English Through Hindi	50.00
G-61	Learn Hindi Through English	45.00
G-100	Learn Arabic Through English	60.00
G-109	Learn Chinese Through English	95.00

JOKES/RIDDLES

G-21	Top Party Jokes	35.00
G-13	1001 Jokes	35.00
G-14	Crazy Jokes	35.00
G-15	Childrens' Jokes	22.00
G-12	Party Jokes	35.00
G-115	The Zanniest Riddle Book	60.00

ESSAY WRITING

G-3	Up-to-date School Essays, Letters and Stories	35.00
G-17	School Essays, Letters & Paragraphs	30.00
G-18	School Essays & Letters For Juniours	25.00
G-30	Selected Essays	40.00
G-96	School Essays, Letters, Paragraphs, Comprehension And Applications	30.00
G-31	Latest Essays	60.00
G-32	160 Essays	95.00
G-50	67 Model Essays	30.00
G-59	Essays For Seniors	35.00
G-71	Advavanced Essays For College & other Competitive Exams.	99.00

LETTER WRITING

G-6	Stolen Love Letters	35.00
G-20	Readymade Letters For All Occasions	65.00
G-38	Improve Your Business Letters	85.00
G-39	350 Model Business Letters	95.00
G-40	Readymade Business Letters	50.00
G-42	Standard Book of Model Letters	45.00
G-44	Lively Love Letters	35.00
G-47	How To Write Impressive Business Letters	65.00
G-48	Top Winning Letters	60.00
G-101	Better Applications For Better Jobs	75.00
G-106	Business Letters For Powerful Communication	75.00
G-124	200 Everyday Letters For All Occasions	45.00

TITLES ON CHESS

G-76	First Moves — How to start a chess game (Foreign Reprint)	45.00
G-77	Pick Up The Best Chess Problems (Foreign Reprint)	50.00
G-79	Basics and Laws of Chess	60.00
G-82	White to Play and Mate in Two (Foreign Reprint)	55.00
G-103	Techniques of Middle Game in Chess	70.00
G-104	Techniques of End Gae in Chess	75.00
G-112	200 Challenging Chess Puzzles	60.00

HEALTH AND FITNESS

G-95	Arthritis	45.00
G-36	Improve Your Eyesight	35.00
G-63	Nature Cure For Common Diseases	60.00
G-64	High Blood Pressure	45.00
G-83	100% Fitness (Foreign Reprint)	50.00
G-121	A Guide To Herbal Remedies	70.00

BABY NAMES

G-46	Goodwill's Book Of Baby Names	45.00
G-85	4500 Baby Names	35.00
G-116	10,000 Baby Names (in two colours)	111.00

GAMES/TRICKS

G-88	101 Classic Magic Tricks (Foreign Reprint)	50.00
G-89	Karate Made Easy (Foreign Reprint)	50.00
G-114	101 Card Tricks (Foreign Reprint)	50.00
G-118	Great Party Games	50.00
G-119	Party Games & Activities For Children	60.00
G-112	Rules & Skills Of Games & Sports	150.00

PALMISTRY, ASTROLOGY NUMEROLOGY

G-90	Cheiro's Guide To The Hand	50.00
G-91	Cheiro's Palmistry For All	60.00
G-93	Cheiro's language Of The Hand	75.00
G-98	Cheiro's Book of Palmistry, Astrology and Numerology	125.00
G-99	Cheiro's You and Your Star	95.00
G-65	Astrology for All	30.00

OTHER GENERAL TITLES

G-49	Readymade Speeches For All Occassions	35.00
G-102	Secret of Success	50.00
G-107	27 Tips For A Super Power Memory	45.00
G-108	How To Succeed In Interviews	50.00
G-4	How To Pass Exams	35.00
G-37	The Book Of Etiquette	40.00
G-53	Noble Thoughts For Better Living	45.00
G-55	Perfect Speaking	50.00
G-70	The World's Great Speeches	60.00
G-69	Common Sexual Problems	35.00
G-81	Management — It's Lighter And Brighter Sides	75.00
G-80	The Power Of Positive Doing (Foreign Reprint)	75.00
G-84	How To Have A Well Mannered Dog (Foreign Reprint)	55.00
G-110	Science Fair Projects With Electricity and Electronics (Foreign Reprint)	75.00
G-120	100 Amazing Make It Yourself Science Projects	70.00

OBJECTIVE SERIES

| G-72 | Comprehensive Objective Botany | 199.00 |
| G-73 | Comprehensive Objective Zoology | 149.00 |